ADVANCED ENOCHIAN MAGICK

A Manual of Theory, Training, and Practice for the Novice and the Adept

Frater W.I.T.

Outskirts Press, Inc.
Denver, Colorado

Advanced Enochian Magick
A Manual of Theory, Training, and Practice for the Novice and the Adept
All Rights Reserved.
Copyright © 2009 Frater W.I.T.
V2.0

Outskirts Press, Inc.
http://www.outskirtspress.com

ISBN: 978-1-4327-3784-9

Outskirts Press and the "OP" logo are trademarks belonging to Outskirts Press, Inc.

PRINTED IN THE UNITED STATES OF AMERICA

TABLE OF CONTENTS

INTRODUCTION

Magick is the key to self empowerment. Its practice opens up doors to a higher state of being, surpassing all human norms. Mages of all times and climes have transcended the human condition by reaching to the heavens or dipping down into the black pits of the underworld. The ardent student of the occult can ascend with the angels to God Most High or command the cohorts of demons to bring wealth, power, and other satisfactions. In all cases, the endeavor is to develop powers that raise one above one's peers, to achieve excellence in a world full of mediocrity and limitations.

The new age in which humanity finds itself offers fantastic, new opportunities for the ambitious wizard to grow and become something far greater than anything yet imagined. What is to come will utterly dwarf everything that has gone before and those positioned to embrace the new mind will be on the vanguard of the evolution of intelligence on this planet. Occult study and practice offers a way to achieve this advanced state of development.

VI · ADVANCED ENOCHIAN MAGICK

The vast literature of occultism reaches to the distant past, through all ages of human existence, and up to the present time. Most of the traditional volumes are couched in religious expressions, which kept the authors safe from inquisitorial persecution. These works tend to be full of blinds and confusions so that only those schooled in the magical traditions of the authors could properly understand what was written. Many unwise occult enthusiasts have taken the deliberate deceptions for literal truth and incorporated them into a mode of practice that led only to illusion and confusion. So many of the unschooled have approached the traditional literature and found nothing but obscurity that the subject as a whole fell into complete discredit for centuries. Those involved with modern science have consigned occultism to the realms of superstition and ignorance, never suspecting that their vaunted materialistic, deterministic viewpoint was blinding them to valuable truths that have been recognized throughout human existence. Not all the mysteries of nature may be apprehended with the intellect.

An attempt to rescue this profound subject was made during the occult revival of the nineteenth and twentieth centuries. Innovative magicians such as S. L. Mathers, Aleister Crowley, and Israel Regardie tried to restore the magical tradition, especially Enochian magick, in a way that made it compatible with prevailing scientific understanding. Their works are respected and widely read even today. Unfortunately, few who approach these books are capable of understanding them as their authors intended. A good deal of study and practice is needed to provide the basic background magical knowledge which Crowley and other occult authors assumed their readers would have.

Many books on magick for beginners have been written to fill this gap. They've been very popular and have sold well over the years. In fact, beginner magick books have come to dominate the market. Few modern works on advanced occultism are to be found in the modern era. There is little interest in them since most enthusiasts rarely get beyond the beginner stage of practice. More advanced magicians have had to consult the old, obscure volumes to try to piece together an understanding of what lay beyond the first ranks of the occult endeavor. This book has been written for those who've achieved more advanced proficiency and are looking for ways to go even further along the path of magick knowledge and power.

The ambitious reader will find chapters on magical theory, emphasizing the Enochian magical path, interleaved with a fast track curriculum of personal training that can raise even beginners to the heights of occult proficiency. The informed and enabled practitioner will then be able to approach the advanced ceremonial work which follows. A foundation will be built that allows access to unlimited sources of wisdom and power at all levels of consciousness and reality. A path leading from mind to matter will take shape as the personal being of the mage expands under the continuing energization of magical understanding and practice. The portal to the inner halls of wizardry is now open.

CHAPTER 1
THEORY

MAGICK IN THE NEW AGE

The modern magician has fantastic advantages over those who've walked this path of mystery in previous ages. The modern sciences of the natural world and the human mind have freed the rational explorer of the occult forces from the superstitions which have confused and limited so many in the past. A vast and wondrous cosmos awaits the touch of the new mind whose scope is realized to be coequal with reality. New vistas of experience are available to one with the courage and Will to move forward into the new age of human realization.

Our grand, new age of wonder and transcendence began with the twentieth century. Advances in art, science, philosophy, and occultism were to propel all of humanity into a complete revisioning of itself, its significance, and its place in the universe. The new mind has developed from the initial explosion of cosmic consciousness into a revelation of personal and impersonal realities which dwarf everything that has gone before. Breakthroughs in galactic astronomy, DNA biology, neuroscience, orgone biophysics, depth psychology, and quantum physics mirror the growing understanding of the human condition as a direct participation in a cosmic process shared by all of life and matter. The scope of possibility has expanded beyond imagination.

Of course, change does not come easily to the human race. Nightmarish world wars were fought which brought much of civilization to ruin. The struggles between the old mind of the slave religious and political paradigms and the new mind of a cosmically realized collective consciousness continue today. Religiously inspired terrorism in every country and economic tyranny throughout the world have brought the human race perilously close to annihilation. The collective unconscious conflict reverberates in each of us, deeply hidden from the awareness of most, yet, right next to us all.

It is into this milieu of enormous possibility, extreme internal and external conflict, and grave risk that today's magician operates, in the world but enjoying a life of communion with the cosmic totality. The period right after the change of an age is rich in opportunity to completely redefine all conceptions and innovate all new modes of life. Communications technology in the 21st century has made information about cultures around the world and throughout the time of human existence widely available. The new age magician can draw together ideas from any number of disparate religious and magical systems to weave novel tapestries of conceptions and practices. Modes of consciousness never before experienced may be explored to suit the blossoming creativity of the new mind.

Ceremonial magick in particular may be used to explore the century old expansion of new consciousness. Archetypal symbols from any culture that has ever existed may be incorporated into the operations of the ritual enthusiast. The deepest of meanings from the collective human unconscious may be associated and blended to generate visions and spiritual communions never before conceived. The modern practitioner enjoys a freedom and a scope of culture never known before. The Celtic Dagda, the Hindu Kali, and the Greek Hades may be invoked at will. Modern scholarship has made available so wide a variety of magical and religious systems that a truly new universe of spiritual exaltation and identification has developed.

Each piece of this colossal tapestry of understanding was thought to be the entirety of existence to those who first believed in and practiced according to its precepts. Now, each is a component in a complex cosmos of experience that encompasses and transcends them. Whole dimensions of psychic operation have unfolded from the collective unconscious in an awesome display of informational expansion. All previous conceptual limitations have disappeared in a new age, which transcends and dwarfs everything that has come before.

New age consciousness has so transcended the current human norm as to allow for the possibility of a futuristic psychic technology. What in the past could only be understood as mysterious spirits and supernatural forces can now be built and operated as psychic machines, products of a technology of consciousness that can reach beyond the boundaries of space and time. The commonly known powers of ESP, such as telepathy, clairvoyance, and precognition are merely the beginning of what will become a whole new way to be a human being. More advanced abilities such as levitation, teleportation, time travel, shape shifting, and production of light and energy are sure to come later. Postmodern wizardry is destined to become a common occurrence for a new race of meta-humans.

All of this will become a reality as ever greater numbers of people come to realize their direct participation in their own creative process, their own inherent divinity. Time will be understood as an ocean rather than an arrow. All limitations will be seen as convenient illusions, to be adopted and dissolved at will. Consciousness will be realized to be the cosmic force that it has always been, focused through and surrounding the individual life form as a field of cosmic concentration onto a particular experience. This is the way the universe can know itself subjectively. The all-encompassing religious theme will be that all that lives is a god in its own right. All that is, is consciousness.

This understanding of how consciousness interacts with matter and energy will enable the development of a psycho-mechanical technology that will advance human living far beyond any previous invention. Machines that are sensitive enough to receive the subtle quantum signal of projection of consciousness and powerful enough to translate that impress of human will into a physically effective force will be able to transform reality according to the intension of the new mind. Space faring technology will be the inevitable product. Vehicles that can carry the human mind to new dimensions of supra-cosmic connectivity, opening up novel astral spacescapes and potentials of experience will expand human consciousness beyond all bounds. First contact with intelligences from beyond our biosphere and dimensional collective will uplift the species to the status of galactic citizens.

This race-redefining gateway event will be yet another in a long chain to follow from the seminal advent of the new age. Evolution will accelerate to a level of complexity that transcends the collective development of species. Each individual human will not only be an independent entity but an individual reality, a personal cosmos interacting with other such novel evolutions. The universe will have blossomed into a myriad of bubble realities, unique and yet whole.

The practice of Enochian magick is ideally suited to launch a person inspired by destiny onto this path toward the ultimate transcendence of the cosmos.

The higher consciousness underlying its revelation was profoundly futuristic for its founder, the Elizabethan magician, John Dee. The experiences which he and his partner, Edward Kelley, had with their angelic contacts indicate the radical nature of their inspirational source. At one point, the mage and his seer were told to swap wives in sexual activity, an idea that was unthinkable in sixteenth century England. It would be centuries before such behavior gained a measure of acceptance.

There is one vision in particular, which Kelley had upon being awakened by the angel, Ave, that spoke across the centuries directly to Aleister Crowley. The transcendent contact revealed a scene with four castles arrayed in a cross pattern, each facing a circle of twenty-four columns. Hosts of angels came out of each Watchtower and marched toward the central circle. Their ranks would later be encoded in the hierarchy of the four Watchtower tablets, from King and Seniors to the servient angels of the subangles.

These very tablets, given elemental and initiatory attributions by the founders of the Hermetic Order of the Golden Dawn, played a crucial role in the training of a young and ambitious occultist named Aleister Crowley. This man received a document four year later that announced the advent of the new aeon, a newly realized access of cosmic consciousness that was to change humanity and society forever. *The Book of the Law* gave details regarding new magical and initiatory formulae, including a telling passage from chapter one, verse 51. It says:

"There are four gates to one palace; the floor of that palace is of silver and gold; lapis lazuli & jasper are there; and all rare scents; jasmine & rose, and the emblems of death. Let him enter in turn or at once the four gates; let him stand on the floor of the palace. Will he not sink? Amn. Ho! warrior, if thy servant sink? But there are means and means. Be goodly therefore: dress ye all in fine apparel; eat rich foods and drink sweet wines and wines that foam! Also, take your fill and will of love as ye will, when, where and with whom ye will! But always unto me."

It seems likely that the four gates refer to the four castles of Kelley's angelically inspired dream vision and the palace is at the center of the twenty-four columns. This is the new palace of initiation at the center of the Enochian universe, not to be revealed to the world until centuries after Dee's and Kelley's time. *The Book of the Law* is a revelation that completes and continues the ground breaking work done by the Elizabethan mages so long ago. Humankind is now ready to begin exploring the new initiatory temple of the far future, guided by the wondrous description given in the above passage. Clues to the significance of the various objects referred to may be found in the Tables of Correspondences in *777 and Other Qabalistic Writings of Aleister Crowley*. There is a new heaven, a new earth, a new religion, and new meanings of life and death for humanity.

Enochian magick can be as transformative for the modern magician as it was for Crowley, Dee, and Kelley. The power evoked by the angelic language and the holographic formatting of its presentation in table and spherical forms continues to beckon us from a distant future state of being. The evolutionary acceleration afforded by its influence on the mind and aura of the practitioner makes Enochian magick ideal for realizing new possibilities of conscious functioning, including the impersonal functions of probability manipulation outside the body. Individual, species, world, and cosmos become one great becoming in a reality of limitless vistas. The future is now with the practice of Enochian magick.

CHAPTER 2
TRAINING

TRACK 1
BEGINNER (NEOPHYTE)

This is the first of three tracks in a training program designed to raise a beginner in the occult arts and sciences to the ultimate of self knowledge and the power that comes with it. The trained magician can access the entire spectrum of personal and impersonal consciousness, from the transcendent heights to the chaotic depths, from the core of being to the edge of the universe and everything in between. Thelemic adepts claim to have their heads above the heavens and their feet below the hells. All spirits, planes, and energies are available to the adept of Hermetic magick, Thelemic or otherwise, whose consciousness has expanded beyond the common realm to reach the limits of possibility and the heart of creation.

Track 1 is designed to introduce the novice in the occult to her or his personal motivations and habits. It is useful to understand where one has been in order to chart the course ahead. Pathways into the depths of the mind begin to be formed and used to prepare for greater work to come. The more one practices magick, the more one can practice magick. A way through the personal mind must be forged before the wonders of the impersonal can be discovered.

What follows is a series of suggested exercises which the reader may undertake if it seems worthwhile. This type of work has been done by many who have taken the Path to self/Self discovery. Of course, the reader is free to pick and choose which if any of these tasks to perform. They have all proven useful to most. However, as in all cases, "Do what thou wilt." This blueprint of personal growth may be adapted to any tradition or magical style, according to the intelligence of the individual. Any number of other exercises may be substituted, which accomplish the same goals as the following. The ambitious magician must always work according to the laws of her or his own being.

Of course, not every magician in training prefers to work alone. There have been some who've seen fit to undergo psychotherapy, particularly of the Reichian school, during their magical training. This can help explorers of the psyche deal with the upwelling hidden contents of their minds, which must be uncovered to pave the way for the revelation of the occult truths which lay beneath. Others, such as the author of this book, have preferred to deal with such personal contents independently. There is greater danger this way but also greater reward. Self mastery is established earlier but some of the buried psychic contents may not be revealed for a long time.

Many have opted for membership in schools of the magical mysteries to seek guidance in their Work. They gain benefit from the greater experience and power of others on the magical Path. However, the magician must give up a measure of control in such settings to receive the carefully guided course of training. This is the safer Path in the beginning because experienced teachers may provide warnings and advice to those who run into trouble along their way. Interaction with other magicians can be very valuable in personal development but it is necessary to submit to the leadership of others who may have agendas that may not take the best interests of their students into account. Some groups are more respectful of the individuality of their members than others.

The author of this book has gone through courses of magical training in two mystery schools as well as made his own way in magick in later years. There is value in doing both individual and group oriented Work but conflicts can arise on such a diverse Path. The novice in occultism must judge the balance of risk and reward in choosing which way to take. Here, then, is a suggested course of training which synthesizes the most valuable Work in the career of Frater W.I.T. It is designed for beginners in occultism who prefer to chart their own course through the dark paths within.

Stage 0:

1. Practice the Lesser Banishing Pentagram Ritual one or two times a day. Add in the practice of the Lesser Invoking Pentagram Ritual when ready.

2. Keep a daily diary of thoughts, experiences, and reactions to magical work. Try to come up with something to write each day for at least the first few months of regular practice. Focus on matters that deal specifically with the magical path of research and training.

3. Do the Thelemic practice of Will before each meal or some such statement declaring that food is being eaten as an aid to accomplishing the Great Work. The practice of Will begins by knocking on a table or some other surface, using the pattern of three knocks, then five knocks, then three knocks, for a total of eleven. Say aloud or to yourself, "Do what thou wilt shall be the whole of the law. It is my Will to eat and drink so that my body may be fortified for the accomplishment of the Great Work. Love is the law, love under Will." Knock one final time and then eat.

4. Perform relaxation practices and fourfold breath exercises. Systematically relax the top of your head, the sides and front of your head, your neck, your shoulders, your arms and hands, your back, your chest, your ab-

domen, your midsection, your anus, and your legs and feet. Focus attention on each part of your body in turn and will the muscles to relax. Slowly begin inhaling for a count from one to four. Hold your breath for four counts. Exhale slowly and carefully for four counts. Hold for four counts. Repeat until complete relaxation is achieved. Alternatively, begin practicing Hatha yoga.

5. Become familiar with a deck of tarot cards. Learn its structure and basic occult correspondences. Read a book or two on the subject. Learn and practice various methods of reading tarot cards. Perform readings for yourself and others.

6. Write an autobiography for yourself. The length and depth of detail are a matter of personal preference. You are writing for yourself. Focus on the significant events of your life, especially those which inspired you to explore occult studies and practices. You may destroy the writing when you're finished or keep it for future reference.

Stage 1:

1. Continue practices 1 through 5 from Stage 0. Yoga enthusiasts may add Pranayama Yoga to their daily routine.

2. Perform the Middle Pillar Exercise once a day.

3. Take up forms of divination other than the tarot which may be of personal interest, such as geomancy, the I-Ching, rune casting, etc.

4. Practice the Greater Pentagram Ritual. Perform one or two rituals for each element.
5. Skry into the Spirit Vision using the five Tattwas. Perform three visions for each of the four elements.
6. Skry the 25 subelements, one or two visions for each.

Stage 2:

7. Continue practices 1 through 3 from Stage 1. Yoga enthusiasts may add Pratyahara Yoga to their daily routine.
8. Keep a separate diary of psychological projections for three months – formulate an understanding of what this is by reading relevant works by Carl Jung and apply this to your daily experiences. Be as detailed as possible. Keep or destroy the work as you see fit.
9. Use the tarot cards to form links between self consciousness and subconsciousness to gain insight into the workings of your hidden mind. Meditate on each of the Major Arcana cards in relation to your own life and mind. Perform readings to explore your personal feelings and motivations.
10. Practice transcendental meditation, a self guided journey into the hidden mind. Systematically relax the body from head to toe and regularize the breathing with the fourfold breath. Visualize walking up a flight of steps, at the top of which is a door. Mentally open the door to see another flight of steps

to ascend. Move through the door and up the steps, at the top of which is another door. Repeat for a third time and, at the top of this, open the door to reveal the vast plane of the hidden mind. Receive whatever images which appear to the mind's eye without judgment or prejudice. After some efficiency is gained in this practice, plant suggestions to change unwanted unconscious behaviors and thought patterns by visualizing a symbol which embodies the changed mindset in your inner psychic space. Do this before going to bed. Record all visions and results in the magical diary.

11. Practice the Lesser and Greater Hexagram Ritual. Perform one or two rituals for each planet and zodiacal sign.

12. Formulate a theory of how consciousness interacts with matter and how the two affect each other. Record all meditations and contemplations in your magical diary. Study the progression of the tarot cards and the Qabalistic Tree of Life for clues, if desired.

The reader should note that the purpose of this curriculum is not to set absolute guidelines that everyone must follow in order to achieve self knowledge and personal power. The fact is that no one has the ability to determine for anyone else how she or he may discover the keys to unlock the mysteries of her or his soul. At best, teachers can show general guideposts along the Path of the Wise. The purpose of this curriculum, therefore, is to provide an example of how one person reached beyond the norm to discover his innermost nature and sources of transcendent power.

Ultimately, each person is her or his own best teacher. The signatures of nature appear differently to each individual and only each can know for herself or himself how best to approach the sublime subtlety of her or his reality. The best scientific minds of the twentieth century have determined unanimously that the nature of the universe is relative to each observer, even to the subtlest realms of existence. There is no absolute reality and so no absolute knowledge. Therefore, it is up to each practitioner to decide for herself or himself how to use the suggestions given in the curriculum.

The course may be followed to the letter or reordered to fit personal preferences. Operations which seem useless or objectionable may be skipped with advantage. The course may be thought of as a salad bar of practices which opens up inroads to transcendent discovery. These activities may be adapted to personal inclination or taken as an example from which to develop a brand new course of action.

The ultimate goal of all true magick is to develop individuality and freedom for each practitioner. All genius and creativity derive at the level of the individual and not from any society, organization, or tradition. A society that exists for the benefit of the individual is the most enlightened and successful.

The Work of Frater W.I.T. is devoted to fostering the creation of such a state of humanity.

Some explanation of the place and purpose of each stage of the suggested curriculum will help the beginner magician to decide how best to approach this track. The specifics of performance of the ceremonies suggested herein may be found in the chapters of this book which are devoted to magical practice.

The purpose of Stage 0 is to introduce the beginner to general magical practices as described in the literature of Western Occultism. The most important ability to be gained along the first stage of the Path is to develop a habit of introspection. Learning to take a step back from personal feelings and motivations opens doorways into the inner recesses of the mind. These hidden depths are the first link between the self and the Beyond. The sources of all Power, all Wisdom, all Love, and all Truth may be found in the vastness of consciousness beyond the personal identity. Working with systems of symbols in an orderly way carries the magician to this state of ultimate transcendence. The most important question to answer at this stage is, why do I want to do Magick?

Stage 1 begins the personal transformation process. The magician undergoes an intensive and exhaustive survey of all the elemental powers as described by the ancient sages of this art. The symbol systems introduced in Stage 0 are internalized and deeply embedded in the subconscious, where most of the real work takes place. Symbols form valuable links between the incarnate self and the transcendent, impersonal reality from which all consciousness and matter depend. They are alphabets which both the self conscious and subconscious minds can understand, each in their own way. They are also conduits of psychic force which the magician must experience and become familiar with. The subtle aura becomes charged and organized by frequent practice. Not only mental but subtle physical changes are initiated in this stage. The body as well as the psyche must be prepared to reach and transmit the charge from the Beyond.

The development of well established links to the inner mind are required to begin Stage 2 work. Accomplishment of the above practices enables success in this. Once the results of subconscious processes become understood, your inner nature may then be discovered and examined. The pathways of magical energy must be purified of self denial and traumatic pain to become effective in transmitting the impress of the Will into manifestation. The mirror of the subconscious may come to reflect higher Truth and greater intensities of power when cleansed of confusion and pain.

Mastery of this track will enable the magician to undertake Track 2 with the greatest confidence. Not only magical work but all of life's endeavors will be enhanced as the barriers of the mind are brought down to allow integration of self consciousness and subconsciousness, producing superconsciousness. A whole new reality awaits a magically expanded mind. Greater effectiveness in mundane affairs will also result. All facets of life will improve.

CHAPTER 3
THEORY

ON THE NATURE OF
INVOCATION AND EVOCATION

The two most basic magical operations are invocation and evocation. All other work ultimately boils down to these two simple functions. However, much confusion about them exists in the minds of many students and practitioners of the occult arts, despite the great body of literature devoted to the subject. The similarities and differences between invocation and evocation need to be clarified so that magicians can perform these operations together or separately to suit their respective needs. Examples of each operation will illustrate just how they fit into the practice of ceremonial magick.

The simple explanation frequently given by teachers of the occult is that invocation calls in, inside of yourself, while evocation calls forth, outside of yourself. The focus of these operations are the vast array of gods and spirits derived from the uncountably many religions of antiquity. Typically, the magician invokes the gods, calling them into her or his being, in order to identify with them and assume their powers. The various angels, demons, and nature spirits are evoked, called through the magician's being, to manifest in the magical workplace as an independently existing creature in order to perform favors for the operator. Confusion arises, however, because many prayers and invocations are used to prepare for the summoning. It can be difficult for anyone unfamiliar with occult literature to keep the two forms of practice in perspective.

These two words, invocation and evocation, are quite similar and they have related meanings. They are both vocations, that is, calls, chants, prayers, speeches. Both types of oration use various names of mythical entities which are called upon to cause some kind of effect. The characteristics of the gods or spirits are declared in order to develop a visualization and related understanding in the mind of the conjurer.

The difference between these types of calling is the intended realm of effect in which the entities are to operate. With invocation, the god enters the mind and inspires the soul of the magician. Every thought, every sensation, the mind's eye, every inner awareness becomes imbued with the presence of the divinity. The body seems to shine with a radiance more felt than seen. The lower spirits are forced to obey the commands of such a god brought into the human realm in this way. With evocation, the spirit manifests in the room with the conjurer.

This arcane presence is as palpable as that from any person or object. Its energies impinge on the nerves the same as from any light or heat source.

The magician may converse with this manifestation from the spirit world the same as with any person. Interaction between conjurer and conjured is like that between master and servant or pet. Unusual effects and occurrences may be achieved through the powers of spirits. They are in essence the projections of the will of the exorcist into the physical world.

These points may be illustrated by considering the following magical systems. The most detailed instruction on invocation can be found in Aleister Crowley's essay, *Liber Astarte*. Exact directions are given for the attitude to be adopted by the magician toward the object of devotion, how the temple of the chosen deity is to be put together, the various meditations and everyday practices to add to the formal ceremonial invocation, and several warnings as to the dangers of this practice. The interested reader may refer to this essay, to be found in *Magick In Theory and Practice*, *Liber ABA*, and *Gems From the Equinox*.

The best known and most popular oration by Crowley to a specific deity is called, *Liber Israfel*. This is a long and detailed invocation of the Egyptian God, Tahuti, Master of magick and writing. The process of devotion to and identification with this deity is clearly indicated in the course of the oration. The many details of the appearance, natural functions, and abilities of the god are mentioned as the magician goes from worship to identification to working magick as Tahuti Himself. The form of the deity is imagined to cover the body of the priest like a garment reaching from head to toe. This image is built up until it subsumes the identity of the devotee. Tahuti takes form in manifestation as the body and mind of the magician, who is lost for a time in the being of the great god. After this intimate contact fades, the blessed mage has gained something special from the deific communion, a permanent increase in psychic, auric, and spiritual energies. S/he is brought that much closer to achieving a divine nature.

The best known example of evocation can be found in that ancient, most popular grimoire known as *The Goetia*. This little book is actually the first of a five part series called, *The Key of Solomon*. The names of 72 demons and their magical sigils are listed. They were supposed to have been imprisoned in a vessel of brass made by the Biblical king and wizard, Solomon. Instructions are given for summoning and controlling these evil spirits so that the good magician may attain any desire and the evil of the world may be bound to the service of God. This was thought to reduce wrong doing in the world and so help bring about peace.

The magician is to stand in a circle of protection, surrounded by divine names written in Hebrew. Several pentagrams and hexagrams are placed inside and outside the circle to add to its protective field. A magick triangle is drawn outside the circle wherein the demon is to appear and be constrained. A divine name is written along each side of the triangle to give it power over the spirits. Several long conjurations are specified, along with vague descriptions of what the demons are like and what they can do. The spirit can be banished once the magician's purpose has been achieved. It can be called back at any time simply by activating its sigil.

In addition to evocation of evil spirits, various systems of angelic evocation were developed for spiritual fulfillment rather than satisfaction of desires. The best known of these is the Enochian systems of magick invented by John Dee in Elizabethan England. He and his seer, Edward Kelley, channeled an angelic language which was structured into tablets and other matrices from which a wide variety of angels' names could be derived. They used prayers and conjurations in the angelic tongue to generate transcendent visions meant to bring the grace of God into their souls. Others have used this language and the various structures of Enochian magick for different purposes but the result has consistently been an uplifting inspiration to a higher state of being. The angels have given a wellspring of information about this world and the greater realm of which the human understanding is but a part.

Dee's angels are easier to deal with than the demons of *The Goetia* but their powers tend to operate in areas transcendent to that of mundane human concern. The magician would find Goetic evocation more useful for finding lost treasure or learning the secrets of adversaries than enlisting the aid of the angels but these lower spirits would be useless for raising the magician's spirituality. Yet, both the angels and demons are dealt with as separate entities outside of the being of the conjurer.

The magical theory behind these types of working is that the names of God or the Gods have intrinsic magical power which no spirit, good or evil, can resist. The wizard can perform an invocation of a god as a preliminary to calling the spirit to appear and obey. All magical traditions assert that knowing the true name of a spirit or god gives one power over that entity. The vast hierarchy of gods, angels, and spirits can be controlled through the use of such names.

The question arises as to the actual nature of these entities. Are they literally real, independently existing persons who are subject to control by certain human speeches or are they simply figments of the human imagination which express our hopes, dreams, and fears? Just what is happening in the magical workplace when the spirit manifests in the triangle, appearing to the consciousness of the exorcist?

The original religious paradigm asserts that a real entity has been called by the magical names. The holy books are literally true, the gods are really in heaven and the demons are really in hell or under-ground. Of course, this fails to explain how two magicians in different parts of the world can conjure the same spirit at the same time and both get results.

Aleister Crowley practiced all of these magical systems and his conclusions can be read in his *Essay on the Astral Plane* found in *Magick In Theory and Practice*. He wrote that there is another magical paradigm that the modern magician can follow, which may be called the psychological paradigm. This world view asserts that the elements of religion and magick stem from ideals in the human psyche, archetypes in the collective unconscious. Magical results are simply a trick of the brain, an illusion resulting from the excitation of the mind caused by ceremonial actions and strange, "barbarous" magical words. The operator generates energized enthusiasm in this fashion to throw her or his consciousness into a frenzy of activity. Other-worldly visions and communications result. Crowley's ultimate conclusion was that it didn't matter what a magician believes in this regard. The important thing is to do the work and record the results.

Other of Crowley's writings assert one or the other paradigm as context and convenience dictated. He wrote in his version of *The Goetia* that the demons were actually parts of the human brain. However, in describing his reception of *The Book of the Law*, his received holy book, he declared that the being who dictated this work is a real entity, a praeter-human individual sent by the Secret Chiefs who watch over humanity to deliver a new religion for a new aeon. Crowley seems to have been at ease in switching back and forth between the two magical paradigms.

The author of this book has practiced Enochian magick for more than ten years now and has come to the conclusion that these spirits begin as psychic ideals and are then projected into physical reality from the mind and nervous system. The mind/brain/body system is brought to a state of extreme excitation by the act of ceremonial magick, with all the ornate regalia and magical sigils, and then acts as a projector which converts psychic energy into a quasi-physical field of effect, including the spirit itself. This manifest magical field can be felt by the magician and others present and everyone can receive mental impressions from the spirit therein. An interdimensional feedback circuit is thus created which can expand consciousness to new realms of sensation. The final result is a psychedelic experience comparable to that explored by researchers such as Timothy Leary, John Lilly, and Terrence McKenna.

With this outlook of magick in mind, the reader can understand the essential difference between angels and demons. Angels are projections of superconsciousness, a concept explored by Aldous Huxley in his essay, *The Doors of Perception*. This Higher and Divine Genius in each person is the oversoul or holistic being in which the entire personal identity exists and is sustained. As such, the higher spirits are emanations of the greater totality of the being of the magician and can uplift the psyche to higher, more complex levels of functioning. Cosmic and super-cosmic awareness can unfold with enough practice.

The demons, on the other hand, are aspects of the magician's subconscious mind, pieces of the personal psyche that are intensified, expanded, and projected before the mind's eye so that they can be examined. They draw from the deep levels of mind, those atavistic mental functions that were used thousands and millions of years ago by our distant ancestors but are now deeply suppressed by the myriads of more modern functions. Evolution doesn't work by replacement, old systems dissolving and being replaced by new systems. The new is developed on top of the old, emerging from the old like a flower growing out of the dirt. The modern human psyche, then, is a vast hierarchy of conscious operations with the oldest circuits still present but overwhelmed by newer and more powerful functions. Demonic evocation resurges these atavisms through the personal content of repressed trauma and rejected feelings to manifest in a magically projected quasi-physical field. The psyche's overall circuit is thus expanded and empowered far beyond the norm.

In conclusion, it may be understood that the difference between invocation and evocation is the area of effect of the magical operation. The magician can become like a god or higher being as an individual or s/he can project the mythical idea into physical reality as a subtle force field, extending the course of conscious feedback beyond the confines of the body and its nervous system. Personal and collective evolution is accelerated by either operation.

CHAPTER 4
TRAINING

TRACK 2
INTERMEDIATE (MAGICIAN)

The practices given in Track 2 training are designed to explore the heights and depths of the unconscious mind as revealed by the Track 1 operations. Success in the endeavors of the beginner track should have taken the magician into the normally hidden domain of consciousness. A path through repressed, traumatic memories and deep seated fears will have been discovered that brings the magician face to face with the vast realm of personal feelings, attitudes, and motivations. The common threads of life experiences stand revealed as stemming from an overall theme of personal identification. The journey undertaken in Track 2 will further explore the newly discovered inner world in order to seek that aspect of consciousness which is beyond personal identification. Success will reveal the impersonal sources of being and becoming which gave birth to the individual and, in fact, all individuals. This is the source of true magical power, touching the commonality of all mind, matter, and energy in the universe.

Stage 3:

1. Continue the regular practices from Track 1 which have proven to be of value. Do them on an ongoing basis throughout the rest of your magical career or for as long as they prove useful. Yoga enthusiasts may add Jnana Yoga and Dharana Yoga to their daily routine.

2. Take up the study of astrology as the science of mapping patterns of human life to the patterns of motions of the stars and planets. Apply this outlook to the study of your natal chart to gain an understanding of the progress of your life in relation to celestial events and patterns. Learn to see the synergy in operation throughout nature as the call of destiny for yourself, the world around you, and the entire universe.

3. Practice astral travel and rising on the planes. Visualize a dark form standing in front of you and transfer the seat of your consciousness to that mental construct. Move around in it and become used to it. Practice this until you can rise out of physical reality into the astral plane. Explore the scenes that appear before your astral senses. When this process becomes easy, practice rising through the astral spaces. Rise upward as much as you can. Don't stop along the way, no matter how fascinating the sights

that appear. Rise until the astral is transcended and you reach a state of dimensionless bliss. This practice can be dangerous so it's wise to proceed slowly.

4. Study patterns in nature, from the shapes and layouts of leaves and flowers to the structure of DNA. Find commonalities among natural objects and relate them to the structures and processes of your mind. Understand natural patterns as the unfoldment of destiny in the realm of its own creation.

5. Study a branch of mathematics that relates to the theories of magick, such as the Qabalah, projective geometry, and topology. See the reading list later on in this book for recommendations for lay readers.

6. Study branches of physics that relate to the practice of magick, such as quantum entanglement, cosmology, superstring theory, the physics of consciousness, and the emergence theories of Ilya Prigogine. See the reading list later on in this book for recommendations for lay readers.

7. Study branches of psychology which relate to occultism, such as the depth psychology of Carl Jung, the character analysis of Wilhelm Reich, and the shadow psychology of James Hillman. See the reading list later on in this book for recommendations for lay readers.

8. Read an encyclopedia of occultism such as Aleister Crowley's *Book 4*, parts 1 through 4, to gain an overall understanding of the

magical tradition. Relate this comprehension to your studies of nature, science, and the synergy of destiny to gain an integrated knowledge of how reality works in life and mind.

9. Gain control of your emotional reactions and become able to reprogram such psychic patterns. Read the works of Dr. Timothy Leary and Dr. John Lilly for insights as to how to accomplish this.

Stage 4:

1. Foster a feeling of passionate love for all life, all events, and all sensations. Realize every experience as a result of the love of the source of existence for every manifestation. Experience destiny as a continual unfoldment of ecstatic love through all structures and processes in personal and impersonal existence.

2. Meditate on the harmony of nature and love in all its forms and expressions. Understand how everything affects everything else in continuous holistic balance and how living beings are the ultimate emergence of order from this background connectivity. Realize how all energy binds together every structure and experience.

3. Meditate on the unity of all life. Discover how your personal life is generated, supported, and maintained by the whole of the biota, the totality of life on earth.

4. Yoga enthusiasts may perform works of Bhakti Yoga. Read Aleister Crowley's *Liber Astarte* in *Magick In Theory and Practice* to find examples of such operations.

Stage 5:
1. Affirm every event in your life as an act of the Will of your Higher Self, especially those phenomena that cause you annoyance or upset. View every experience as a direct communication from the Holy Guardian Angel. Become partners in creation with the universe, from its very beginnings through the present time and into the indefinite future.

2. Integrate all the knowledge gained over the course of this training so far and formulate your personal True Will based on this in a short, simple sentence. This formula should be sufficient to explain every detail of your life and motivations past, present, and future. Let this be your guide in all subsequent experiences. An example of this is the Will formula of Aleister Crowley, "To teach the next step." The next step is the law of Thelema and the relevant magical initiation processes.

3. Help others to achieve magical advancement by teaching classes, writing about and publishing your magical experiences, or supporting a magical organization.

4. Achieve a direct perception of the flow of cosmic creative energy through your being.

This can manifest as a rise of Kundalini up your spine, a continuing consciousness of the presence of the entire universe all around you and within you, an expansion of consciousness leading to impersonal love for all of reality, etc.

5. Achieving the Yogic trance of Dhyana is relevant to this stage.

6. Perform the Thelemic Adept Self Initiation Ceremony as described in a later chapter or some variant thereof that establishes you as a true adept of magick. This should be the culmination of the training course so far.

Stage 3 guides the practitioner to the next level of contact with the unconscious. The natural connection with transpersonal realities may be explored once personal expressions of consciousness become integrated and harmonized. Intellectual exercises have been found to broaden the mind to ideas beyond the obvious reality as reported by the bodily senses. Physical science has always been an integral part of magick. Its study yields great benefits to minds seeking expansion. However, the magician must keep in mind that knowledge is only useful in so far as it points the way to a higher state of being.

Stage 4 is very simple, yet difficult to accomplish. The key idea here is love, not in the ordinary sense but in a way that reaches beyond the bounds of normal conscious reality. Impersonal love lifts the total psyche to transcendent joys, fostering pure ecstasy. Attainment of participation in the steady stream of cosmic love is unmistakable and will transform one's reality in fantastic, unexpected ways. Success in this is one of the most important achievements in the entire course of training. Everything that has been done to this point is meant to enable the breakthrough into impersonal love and unity. All magick power derives from this transpersonal function.

Stage 5 is also simple, yet difficult to accomplish. The key here is integration, bringing together all the lessons, experiences, connections, and energizing love gained in the training course. Success requires more than memory, more than understanding of inner processes. The expanded psyche must be forged into a single focused entity, equally invested in the myriad planes of the mind and cosmos, within and surrounding the body, and through the intervening dimensions of being. The total individual must be guided by a single purpose whose import encompasses all of life and transcends it. The gateway to the racial and cosmic levels of consciousness is made open to the accomplished adept. The mysteries of life are resolved into crystal clarity for such an enlightened, empowered, integrated person. Advanced practices of magick may be undertaken with utmost confidence.

CHAPTER 5
THEORY

UNDERSTANDING AND GENERATING MAGICAL POWER

"Consciousness is the power of magick." This quote from my previous book, *Enochian Initiation*, follows from my definition of magick as the process of projecting psychic energy into physical reality. The extraverted meditation that is ceremonial magick involves the use of archetypal symbols such as the wand, cup, dagger, and disk to excite the mind and nervous system of the operator to the point where a new breakthrough of consciousness is achieved. This energized enthusiasm can then be focused through the aura to project a field of reified psychic energy throughout the temple space. The various angels, elementals, and spirits can take form anywhere along the path of magical projection and express the many facets of the magician's mind. Their visions and verbal communications can provide new information about the practitioner's life and permanently expand her or his psychic course.

Archetypes affect the mind by causing its many functions to act together under the same influence. The images, sounds, sensations, and motions of ceremonial magick are so basic to human experience that every part of the psyche reacts in unison to their input. Processes which cut across the entire spectrum of consciousness grow from these archetypal seeds.

Ego based awareness begins to gain access to the actions and reactions of the unconscious, normally deeply repressed over a lifetime's effort to deny them. This is the reason why so many run screaming from the door to initiation, the reason why every exoteric religion has vilified this most exalted and valuable endeavor. It is a herculean effort to face the myriads of fears, traumatic memories, and shame infused feelings so deeply buried in the struggle to live up to parental and societal expectation. The daring magician must learn to manage her or his psychic constitution and behavior in a new way to continue the process of integration of consciousness. Psychotherapy can be a great help in working this phase of magical training.

Success in this journey through personal darkness brings fantastic rewards. Marvelous ecstasy and pure wonder dawn like a blazing sun in the mind of the one who clears away the emotional blocks and self denial that bring so much misery to life. A whole new function of consciousness evolves from the fusion of hidden psychic contents and the operations of self awareness. New dimensions of reality unfold within the being of the transcendent mage, bestowing the ultimate in beatific and holistic communion. New avenues of control over the forces of life and existence become available to the adept in the art magick. A whole new way to exist is realized.

Various writers have referred to this advanced mode of being as superconsciousness and impersonal consciousness. It is the gateway to power and joy beyond the imaginations of the norm. The walls which appear to divide the self from the universe gradually come down, enabling personal desire to be impressed upon reality directly. The microcosm of personal being joins with the macrocosm of the impersonal totality that is the source of all consciousness and matter. Legendary psychic and magical powers eventually come to the true adept.

The magical tradition describes several different roadmaps for the journey to the innermost self and the outermost reality. The Qabalah specifies thirty-two steps which lead from normal waking consciousness to the core source of all existence. These are the ten Sephiroth and the twenty-two Paths of the Tree of Life. The science of alchemy stipulates a program of Solve et Coagula, divide and recombine, to be done over and over again until the target of the operation is perfected. Hindu mystical philosophy describes seven primary chakras, energy centers of the aura, placed along the spine. Activating each one from lowest to highest brings about the heights of enlightenment.

Modern day magicians can benefit from lore from all across the ancient world. They can also take advantage of the profundity of modern science that has developed since the start of the new age, especially psychology, quantum physics, and cosmology. Answers to the oldest questions about life, humanity, and existence have been given by modern researchers in a realistic way that isn't bound by superstition and dogma.

Carl Jung has outlined his theory of archetypes of the collective unconscious. A great deal more about the makeup and operations of the human mind is understood as a result. Wilhelm Reich has described his research into the cosmic and sexual forces of orgone. The universal nature of impersonal consciousness as the root of human identity is thus more firmly rooted in a rational scientific framework. This is merely the beginning of the development of a detailed description of the physics of consciousness.

For magical and initiatory purposes, however, the most useful modern theory of the workings of the human mind was developed in the 1960s by the psychologist and political activist, Dr. Timothy Leary. He developed a map of the mind called the Eight Neural Circuit model. These eight stages chart the evolution of consciousness from the earliest life forms through the current state of humanity and into the distant future, involving human existence in outer space. The first four circuits deal with how consciousness has adapted to life on earth while the last four functions deal with the necessities of existence off world. It is these latter four psychic evolutions that chart the development of magical training.

Leary believed that these "post terrestrial" circuits could be developed here on earth with the carefully applied use of psychedelic substances, LSD in particular. Not only could the basic psychic powers such as levitation, telepathy, and clairvoyance be evolved in communities of advanced individuals but also more futuristic ideals such as DNA manipulation, control of subatomic processes, and creation of black holes and new universes. His own work with psychedelics seems to have given him a profound understanding and prescience of where humanity is headed in this new age of self awareness and cultural emancipation. However, he wouldn't admit that many of the topics on which he expounded had direct relevance to age old magical subjects such as alchemy, synchronicity, and spirit evocation.

An exploration of Leary's Eight neural circuits, with their cultural and mystical relevance, will provide an understanding of how one might approach this course of personal growth in ways that differ from Leary's own modes of operation. The 1st circuit is called the biosurvival circuit. This refers to the conscious functioning of the simplest living organisms and to the most basic of human instincts such as those of an infant. The 2nd circuit is called the territorial circuit. This charts the development of the more advanced animal instincts such as territorial concerns, locomotion, and emotions. The fight or flight instinct is also involved. The functioning of young children is indicated. The 3rd circuit is called the manual – laryngeal circuit. This is the tool and symbol making stage. Intellectual functioning has evolved, enabling human cultural development and speech. The teenage mind is indicated. The 4th circuit is called the social – sexual circuit. This involves incorporation of the individual into a formal societal structure wherein procreation is devoted to maintenance of the group. Rigid social and religious norms are established to control individual actions and maintain the status quo. Contemporary mainstream culture has fulfilled this last of the terrestrial functions. Government tyranny and war result from the understanding that terrestrial existence is absolute.

The breakthrough into the post terrestrial circuits begins with a sudden emancipation from cultural norms and attachments. Such an event occurred in the early years of the 20th century. The revelation of a new level of conscious functioning brought radical developments in the arts, sciences, and religion, which overthrew cultural patterns that had been adhered to for hundreds and in some cases thousands of years. A great new age had dawned on humanity that promised to completely transform the species.

Biologists refer to such radical shifts in evolution as gateway events. Previous gateway events include the developments of speech, agriculture, and city building. The latest gateway event of cosmic conscious realization had opened an entirely new reality of human understanding and interaction. The two world wars and subsequent conflicts are only some of the shock waves initiated by this quantum leap in the evolution of consciousness.

The rock and roll music revolution of the 1950s involved a cross cultural fusion of American white, middle class ideals and rural African American artistic inspiration. The rhythm and blues music that had been celebrated for decades by African Americans in the southeastern United States began to be enjoyed by white kids all across the country. Habits, language, and mannerisms considered unacceptable by mainstream society were adopted wholeheartedly by a generation of teenagers who came to appreciate new influences from many different sources.

Naturally, their parents objected strongly to these outside influences. They wanted their children to be copies of themselves and maintain the traditions of society without question or hesitation. However, once the intelligence genie was out of the bottle, there was no going back to the old age. Cultural fusion among American subgroups broke a generation of young people out of the 4th circuit of hive America. A rare breakthrough in consciousness was achieved on a national level, beginning a spiritual revolution like none ever heard of before. American blues music spread throughout the world and inspired young people in many countries to take up the art. Musicians with a message of peace, love, and acceptance of different cultures began to change the world forever.

This destiny altering 5th circuit is called the neuro-somatic circuit. The mind and body are seen as part of an independently existing time and space ship. The individual is a uniquely experiencing entity with a destiny independent of others. Elements of different cultures could be mixed and matched according to pleasure and interest. Many taboo subjects such as sex, occultism, recreational drugs, and primitive behavior came to be indulged in without concern for divine punishment or societal ostracism. Leary called such people hedonically enlightened.

A way forward toward profound evolution of consciousness had been revealed. All the efforts of the moral arbiters of society, the politicians, clergy, and police, were unable to stem the tide of the new mind, though their reactionary backlash was severe and destructive. Many suffered and were falsely imprisoned for their advocacy of the new freedom, including Leary himself, but the masses of future directed, meta-cultural, hedonic seekers would not be intimidated. Leary coined a term to describe such people. They are future-unique, futique, which is opposite to antique, of the old way. The futique are leading humanity to peace, intelligence, and outer space.

This advance in consciousness is exactly what a magician achieves upon successfully purging her or his mind of subconscious blocks. The psychic integration of the strata of the personal self, so well described in Jung's depth psychology, leads the healed individual to cultural and circumstantial independence. This coagula that follows the solve of magical training leaves the practitioner with a profound level of freedom and opens the way toward the next step, the revelation of impersonal consciousness. Dr. Leary envisioned this adept stage in his mind map as the 6th neural circuit..

The 6th circuit is called the neuro-electric circuit. The nervous system becomes so intimately integrated with the psychic fusion of the 5th circuit as to act as a sensory organ, a vast antenna system. Signals of cosmic scope are received and made available to the mind, providing the first inkling of impersonal consciousness. The force that takes shape as personal identity among the myriad processes of the brain is directly experienced as a cosmic scale essence which is focused onto an individual perspective. It is understood that the body doesn't generate or contain consciousness but rather conducts it like a wire conducts electricity.

The resulting expansion of personal awareness reaches to the totality of humanity, what Jung called the collective unconscious. A higher love for all people has been frequently reported by users of LSD as well as by devoted monks and mystics who've attained advanced states of spiritual transcendence through long years of practicing rigorous disciplines. Psychedelic drugs make the process happen faster but less reliably. No control is possible and the experience can go either way, to the transcendence or to the personal hell of the deep subconscious. It's like sitting on a bucket of dynamite and then lighting the fuse to see how high the user can be blown. However, doors open that never close again. Carefully guided usage in favorable settings with a spiritual mindset can provide a worthwhile path to the ultimate transcendence.

Direct awareness of the highest human destiny dawns on the mind so excited by these and other methods of attainment. Leary himself claimed to have learned more about the human mind from a five hour psilocybin experience than in his previous twelve years as a professional psychologist and tenured professor at Harvard. Unfortunately, some have had very negative experiences under the influence of LSD, a bad acid trip. Albert Hoffman, the inventor of LSD, compared his "problem child" to psychic dynamite. As usual, the reactionary forces of government oppressed the psychedelic movement and banned all possession and use of the drug. Some states of mind are simply too threatening for political leaders to accept.

Few futiques have ever made it passed this exalted function of the mind, brain, and nervous system. Leary, however, was able to discern a yet more advanced level of meta-psychic operation. The 7th neural circuit is called the neuro-genetic circuit. The integrated mind and brain have become so attuned to the subtlest frequencies of living energies as to become aware of signals coming from the DNA within every cell in the body. Leary refers to DNA as pure information. He identified a metaphysical presence with the double helix of molecules carrying the baseline data on which the entire complexity of the human body is built. His psychedelic journey had led him from the innermost to the outermost and back to his immediate presence.

A whole new set of genetic functions becomes available to a fully actualized 7th circuit futique. Cloning technology is a sign of 7th circuit understanding. Brand new life forms can be produced with this level of control. An occultist might recognize the description of an alchemical homunculus or a Qabalistic golem. Genetic memory is another example of psycho-neuro-genetic functioning. Repressed experiences from prior states of evolution become accessible to personal awareness. These atavisms may be further resurged by using spirit evocation. A host of magical powers has been reported to become available to the advanced adept and the futique operator.

One more stage of evolutionary advance in consciousness has been described. The 8th circuit is called the quantum-gravitational circuit. The principle of personal consciousness has become emancipated from the limitations of organic matter to enter a cosmic scale existence. The being of such a transcendent master becomes fully invested in the cosmic forces first revealed in the 6th circuit. Black holes can be directly manipulated with the gravitational control imposed by such an advanced will, a direct manipulation of the fabric of spacetime. The more familiar magical powers involved with this superhuman mode of being are materialization and dematerialization at will, levitation, telekinesis, and teleportation. Time and space, mass and energy, are as clay in the hands of such a super being.

Ultimately, new universes could be created by one fully attained in psycho-neuro-genetic-quantum integration. Perhaps this cosmos is the creation of such a fully actualized being who evolved in another reality. It may be that this circuit isn't even the last stage that can be evolved. There could be many rungs on the ladder to the ultimate transcendence, each with its own set of eight or more stages of development. Existence may extend far beyond what can be perceived or imagined at this stage of human evolution.

The amazing truth that can be seen from this grand path of perfection is that the mind has the ability to examine itself in unlimited detail. It can trace its own growth and evolution from the beginnings of life to the ultimate potential of its becoming. All of time and space is the mind's playground. It has no limits except those it chooses to focus itself onto. The hallmark of consciousness is its unique ability to step into and out of its own conditions at will, establishing a complex hierarchy of relationships which reaches all the way to the cosmic scale. The universe expands continually under the influence of its own transcendent processes. Far from evolving toward a null state of heat death, as classical physics asserts, the cosmos is striving toward ever increasing complexity, ever increasing intelligence. Just so, human consciousness is evolving in the same way.

Dr. Leary has given an important clue as to the nature of this process of self complexification. He referred to DNA as pure information and the genetic code is an evolving system of memory which builds itself based on its previous states of complexity. It is a form of consciousness like the psyche and the cosmos. Such self referential systems use themselves as the basic template upon which to build new structures and processes. This is why evolution works by superposition, new functions emerging out of preexisting processes, and not replacement of the old by the new.

The structure of the human brain is an example of self referential development. The most primitive parts are placed on the bottom while the cerebral cortex, the most advanced structure, which enables the information processing responsible for human intelligence, is placed on top. Following the same pattern, the old cultures of the previous age still exist among humanity, even though new age consciousness has come to the fore in the more advanced societies. The clash between these radically different mindsets continues to be played out on the international stage.

The myriad forms of life on earth and other self referential systems evolve in similar patterns. The laws of information, excellently represented in the science of mathematics, are followed throughout the universe. The patterns of galaxy formation mirror the structures of seashells and hurricanes. The different types of matter and the different forces involved in these systems conform themselves to the same basic patterns of self referential growth.

One mathematical conception which appears repeatedly throughout the natural world is the Golden Mean proportion. The lesser part is to the greater part as the greater part is to the whole. This natural proportion is approached by a series of numbers discovered by the Italian mathematician, Leonardo Fibonacci. Each number is the sum of the previous two numbers in the series. These numbers are realized by growth patterns throughout the biological world, especially the rings of petals that grow on flowers. These patterns are direct materializations of pure information, just as each body expresses its underlying DNA sequences.

Mathematics can be used in this way to model the complex processes growing out of the ever expanding evolution of self referential systems of pure information such as the psyche and DNA. Topology is a branch of mathematics that is particularly useful in studying these types of consciousness. Relationships between states of being of any type may be modeled as geometrical structures. The most abstract concepts may be represented this way. Study of the relationships of such topological forms suggest novel ways to consider the body of information being modeled.

Self referential systems may be modeled topologically with a geometrical figure called a torus. This is a basic donut shape. Take a circle and then rotate it around a point next to it through the third dimension. A torus is a circle of circles, a wheel of wheels. The various curves that can be drawn on its surface represent the flow of information in a self referential system. A line through the center of the ring of circles can never be reached by any of these curves. This is a good metaphor for the Higher Self implied by the action of the ego. A leap out of the system is needed to attain the transcendence.

There is an illustration representing a four dimensional torus in a book called, *The Mathematical Tourist* by Ivars Peterson. It is shown as a series of concentric tori, each layered on top of the others. A cross section of this object shows its many internal layers. Each 3-D torus represents a system of personal identity, a set of related associations which defines a segment of personality. Jumping out of this system to a higher level of consciousness is to reach a higher level of torus containing the transcended identification. An actual four dimensional torus would have an infinite number of three dimensional tori within it, just as a line has an infinite number of points in it. This indicates that there is no limit to the possibilities of expansion of consciousness. Each leap to the next higher torus level expands the totality of being of personal identity. Leaping also to the innermost axis of this wheel of wheels unites all of consciousness with its origins in space and time. The most complete fulfillment may be experienced by this unlimited process.

The torus model has cosmological uses as well. Modern theories state that our universe is shaped like a saddle. It is remarkably flat and may either expand forever under the original impetus of the Big Bang creation or eventually shrink back to its original point dimension under the force of gravity. The intriguing fact is that the saddle shape is part of the surface of a torus. The thirty Enochian aethyrs which surround the central cube of the Watchtowers of the material universe, like layers of an onion, exemplify the pattern of holistic toroidal expansion. They are expansions of cosmic consciousness accessible to human adept awareness. Wisely have the ancient sages claimed that Man is a microcosm, a little universe. The complex self referential information process is the same. Each act of magick projects the totality of the magician onto the surrounding universe, creating an new holistic level of information complexity. Reality warps under such influence.

Similarities in form and function throughout nature have been studied by scientists and natural philosophers for centuries. One of the most important alchemical doctrines is the existence of natural signatures and correspondences. All material forms derive from a few ideal archetypes or signatures so that similar objects have an inherent connection with each other. These correspondences can be manipulated directly in order to transmute base materials into their perfected forms. Transmutation of lead into gold is one example of this principle.

Certain modern scientists have also recognized this occult truth. The Nobel prize winning physical chemist, Ilya Prigogine, understood that the same few forms tend to emerge from natural chaos. He described them using the word archetype. The particular materials and forces involved in the chaos don't effect what type of structure takes shape as the level of order increases under certain conditions. The structures of emergent order fall into three broad categories: waves, spirals, and dendrites. The soliton waves that cross entire oceans, hurricanes, and the structure of brain cells are examples of these wide ranging patterns.

F. David Peat discusses the relationships that exist between apparently unrelated events to develop his theory of synchronicity. All events occurring at the same time express the state of the universe as a whole at that moment. Reality involves a cosmic coherence, even though there are no causal connections between most synchronous events.

Natural archetypes are emerging all the time according to Robert Laughlin. He describes the process of crystal production in his book, *A Different Universe*. It is very difficult to create a new kind of crystal, one with a different molecular structure than any other. However, it becomes easier to remake the same type of crystal once it is initially created. This has been verified in laboratories across the world.

The novel structure can be recreated with greater ease with each repetition.

This process mirrors the development of new ideas in human thought. Human collective archetypes are one subclass of natural archetypes intrinsic to reality. The evolution of consciousness is at the forefront of the emergence of cosmic complexity. This is the function that human existence performs in the scheme of things.

A special balance of order and chaos is required for the emergence of higher order out of chaos and the development of new natural archetypes. The physicist, Murray Gell-Mann, explores this topic in his landmark book, *The Quark and the Jaguar*. There must be an equal balance between the regularities in a material system and the chaos therein in order for complex information systems such as biological structures and consciousness to emerge.

This balance between order and chaos is a vital part of a branch of mathematics called fractals. A fractal is a wondrous object with unlimited detail and a nearly perfect geometrical order. Yet, it also has a natural, organic look as well. These forms have been used to model a wide variety of natural forms and processes and for computer modeling of realistic situations such as video games. John Briggs describes how much of the natural world comes together in fractal patterns in his book, *Fractals: The Patterns of Chaos*.

A fractal is generated on a computer based on a seed equation. It is a self recursive equation, which means that its output is then used as the next input. Each seed number is given a color based on whether the self recursive process eventuates in a rise to infinity, a fall to zero, or a repeating oscillation between two or more numbers. Millions of seed points in a fixed range are calculated and then plotted on a screen. The result is a multicolored wonder of geometric regularity intertwined with pure chaos. Various organic patterns may be found among the whirls and lines of repeating shapes. The more closely such a figure is examined, that is, the narrower the range of seed numbers, the more detail emerges.

What makes fractals true wonders is that the overall top level shape appears in odd spots at all levels of detail. This characteristic mirrors how the cosmic totality exists at all scales of size within itself. It is contained by what it contains, a paradoxical state that is the hallmark of holograms. Some scientists such as David Bohm have reached the conclusion that the universe is a vast, moving hologram, an unlimited hierarchy of unfoldment of nature wherein every system interacts with every other. The whole is in each and every part. There is perfect feedback of energy and information flowing throughout the cosmic system. This holomovement is a true mirror for human consciousness. As the Hermetic philosophers say, "Deus est Homo."

Each new complexity that develops from this global/local feedback is propagated throughout the universe. Each new balance of order and chaos increases the likelihood of that novelty occurring again in material expression. Thus, the universe is a patterned complexity generator with individuated consciousness as the greatest complexification. This is how an enhanced human mind can influence events not immediately connected to the nervous system. The nature of reality can change under such power. Magick is the ultimate of life, the highest reality in reality.

The sciences of information have revealed a great deal about the functions of consciousness, its place in nature, and its ultimate potentials for advance. Consciousness is a profound example of emergent order, a phenomenon found throughout the natural world. This grandest complexity is part of greater collectives at the species, planetary, stellar, galactic, cosmic, and supercosmic levels of reality.

Yet, human awareness, with its myriad associations of personal experiences as well as collective inspirations, is not a hurricane, a seashell, or a galaxy. Its complexities and speed of operations are at a level that completely dwarfs all other natural forms of emergent order. An inquiry into the anatomy and function of its material basis, the brain and nervous system, will increase understanding as to the exceptional nature of this metaphysical principle.

Physicists are finally addressing the question of consciousness after centuries of ignoring the problem. The classical physics of the old age assumed that the faculty of human awareness had nothing to do with material phenomena. It existed in a reality apart from matter and energy and so could be disregarded by the inquiry into the laws of nature. Descartes' philosophy of mind-body division was accepted without question until the advent of quantum physics in the new age.

Quantum mechanics is the single most verified scientific theory is history. Its predictions match experimental results to within one part in a hundred trillion. Yet, the physics of the ultra small fails to account for how any large scale objects such as desks, cars, and people can exist. Many physicists have theorized that the consciousness of the observer somehow brings objects of the material world of normal human experience into being from the mass of indefinite possibilities predicted by quantum physics. Nothing in the new theory can account for this transition to certain probability.

Some physicists such as Roger Penrose have looked for answers to the question of how consciousness affects reality by studying the minute details of neural anatomy. Penrose reports in his book, *Shadows of the Mind*, that nerve cells are lined with a network of tiny tubes, microtubules, which may act as superconductors. These allow for the quantum transitions of conscious action to take place.

A superconductor allows electrons to move through it without resistance. The tungsten filament in a light bulb radiates light and heat because of its resistance to the electrical current flowing through it. Likewise, copper wire gets hot when electricity flows through it. Energy from the electrons of a current is lost in this way because of resistance. A superconductive material has no resistance and so no energy from electrical current running through it is lost. The unusual properties of a superconductor enable electrons to exist in the same quantum state, that is, they all act as if they were one particle. The randomness of normal current that leads to resistance doesn't exist in this state. Quantum effects such as quantum leaps from one state, position, momentum, etc. to another are expanded to the large scale in this way. Physicists use to term quantum coherence to refer to this expansion beyond the ultra small scale. Such quantum leaps outside a particular state of mind characterize human consciousness.

Structures of microtubules have been discovered on the surface of many types of cells in nature. These may be what give awareness to the smallest of living creatures. The collective action of billions of such superconductive filaments is quite possibly what enables individuated consciousness on the human scale. Quantum effects are expanded to the level of the entire brain in a multidimensional, complex feedback hierarchy

Magical integration continues the quantum coherence expansion to encompass all the cells in the body, the DNA therein, and beyond to other quantum systems. If all emergent order in the universe involves quantum coherence to a greater or lesser extent, including the universe as a whole, then incorporation of planetary, stellar, galactic, cosmic, and supercosmic consciousness with an enhanced individual intelligence is inevitable.

Leary's neural circuits are leaps of neural quantum coherence, which reach to the innermost core of life and the outermost reaches of existence. The correlation signatures by which all natural order is guided become integrated into the set of psychic archetypes which shape the enlightened mind. Control of material and psychic archetypal patterns leads to all of the legendary magical powers and the abilities predicted by Dr. Leary. Matter, energy, space, time, and consciousness can be ordered according to the wizard's will. Nature and artifice become one.

CHAPTER 6
TRAINING

TRACK 3
ADVANCED (ADEPT)

The magician who has integrated the presence of the cosmos in her or his mind, nervous system, and aura can truly be called an adept. An adept is one who understands the force of destiny in all events, thoughts, and actions and can control these flows of reality by an act of Will. Magical ceremonial can be useful in focusing and honing the adept's Will but is no longer necessary for the adept to impose an imprint of Will onto the objective universe. Such a transcended one can weave new symbol systems to express new archetypes of cosmic comprehension and action. The adept is now capable of guiding herself or himself with utmost confidence, following an individual track particularly suited to the adept's needs and nature. The veils of symbols have been drawn back to reveal the Truth beyond the Light, beyond light and darkness, beyond fear and hope, beyond the fickle finger of fate.

What follows can be no more than general suggestions, covering the main systems of advanced occult
practice. The adept is fully capable of deciding what
directions in magick to take, having fulfilled the
ancient charge to know yourself. That truth of
self/Self can be eloquently expressed as "Deus est
Cosmos est Homo."

Stage 6:
1. Develop a system of magical symbols that
   describes the cosmos according to your personal realizations about yourself, reality, and
   the interaction between the two. Develop
   ceremonies to put this magical system into
   action.
2. Undertake a complete course of Enochian
   angelic evocation such as that described in
   Enochian Evocation by Frater W.I.T. Evoke
   the six Seniors and then the King of each
   elemental Watchtower tablet in turn. The
   five Spirit angels from the Tablet of Union
   can complete this comprehensive Work. Following the initiatory order of Earth, Air,
   Water, Fire, and Spirit can effectively reca-
   pitulate your personal course of growth on a
   higher and more intense level of operation.
   Unresolved issues can be worked out from
   this greater perspective. This work can be
   extended by the advanced evocation ceremonies given in the Practice chapters of this
   book. Evoke the 30 Aethyrs from the 30th to
   the 1st.

3. Evoke demons from the medieval grimoire known as *The Goetia*. Other grimoires may also be consulted.

4. Make talismans for specific purposes or for general acceleration of personal magick power. Gather a group of magicians to create a talisman for collective purposes. Each participant can bring her or his own talisman, to be consecrated along with that of the group to take advantage of the greater source of power for personal work.

5. Perform an Abramelin working, following the instructions given in the grimoire of that name or the abbreviated instructions as given in the 8th Aethyr vision of Aleister Crowley's *The Vision and the Voice*. Achieve the knowledge and conversation of the Holy Guardian Angel. Create talismans according to the instructions given in part three of *The Book of the Sacred Magic of Abramelin the Mage*.

6. Evoke the dark forces, such as the Qliphoth of the Tree of Life and the zodiacal signs, the twenty-two spirits given in Aleister Crowley's *Liber 231*, etc.

CHAPTER 7
THEORY

THE MAGICAL SIGNIFICANCE
OF THE PYRAMID

The pyramid has been featured in one way or another in every magical system known to humanity. Its four lines rising from the corners of its square base to a common point directly above the center of the base has always represented a passage from the rectilinear world of humankind to a transcendent state of being. The pyramid has ever been a gateway between earth and heaven, between this life and the afterlife, between this world and the otherworld. Its use in ancient Egypt as a tomb structure and a magical space wherein humans and the gods could meet began a long tradition of usage of its geometry in the western mysteries.

A significant example can be found in the adaptation of the Enochian system of magick made by the Hermetic Order of the Golden Dawn in the late nineteenth century. The founders of this innovative group envisioned each square of the elemental

Watchtower tablets to be truncated pyramids. Each side of these 156 x 4 pyramids, plus the 20 of the Tablet of Union, was given various attributions based on their positions in this idealized model of the magical universe. There is no apparent reason why the chiefs of the Golden Dawn designed their adaptation of John Dee's premiere magical system in this way but their design has become the de facto standard for much of the occult community. This usage not only allows for the derivation of many angelic names from the tablets but also each individual square may be used as the center for a system of symbols to be skried and meditated upon. A whole symbolic universe may be explored in exquisite detail at the level of the square, the quadrant, and the tablet.

A study of the geometry of the pyramid will reveal the reasons for its inclusion in so many magical systems which seek a symbolic picture of the material universe united with the magical universe of the gods, angels, elementals, and demons. As described above, the pyramid consists of a square base and four triangles, resulting in a figure of five sides, five points, and eight edges. A commonly used variation is the ziggurat, which consists of gradually shrinking, concentric, squares rising from a base of maximum size. The magical significance is the same as the Egyptian style pyramid, an artificial mountain whose interior spaces hold temples, tombs, and initiatory rooms. It is no accident that the mountain of initiation of the Rosicrucians, Mount Abiegnus, is called a mountain of caverns.

The top point is the transdimensional gateway connecting the material and astral worlds. The descent
from that summit to the square base is the descent
of the magical, deific nature toward the earth. The
base itself forms the place where deity and humanity may first meet, the square having been frequently used throughout history as the primary
symbol for terrestrial reality. The subterranean
vaults below the pyramid show the influence of the
creative principle in operation through all the underlying forces of human existence and experience,
including death. This is the place of the demons of
the underworld.

All of the operations and forces of magick are represented by this august structure, including the creation of the universe itself. The force that causes
changes in events and consciousness to occur in
conformity with Will is the force that brought the
cosmos into being from the nothingness that is
every possibility, called the Ain Soph Aur in the
Qabalah. The emergence of this cosmic Will from
the All/Naught can be conceived of as the formation
of a specific point in the midst of the homogeneous
field of pure potential. The Self-created Will-Point,
reflected in the personal Wills of all that lives, is
called Kether in the Qabalah and is that very point
at the top of the pyramid which connects this world
and the otherworld. The focusing of the Primordial
Point out of the infinite sea of All/Naught is the first
break in the symmetry of the potential field. A
process of symmetry breaking and further specifica-

tion has begun that will eventuate in the creation of the material world and every living creature therein.

The second symmetry break occurs as the first focal Point undergoes a projection of Itself in a particular direction, the first specified direction in the universe. A line forms, extending outward from the Point in two directions, so that the original is always at the midpoint. The running and returning of the Point in infinite motion constitutes the first dimension of existence, the first continuum of possibility. This state is called Chokmah in the Qabalah.

The line meets itself at the point of ultimate extension from the original, establishing the truth that extremes meet. The Primordial Point is now projected infinitely in a specific domain of possibility. The first line now exists in infinitely many orientations, establishing an infinite variety of linear dimensions. The interrelations between all points and lines in infinite motion forms the first triangle in every possible orientation. The Point is one with the line that is one with the circle/triangle. This state is called Binah in the Qabalah.

The third symmetry break occurs as the first line projects itself in a way that doesn't intersect with itself. The line projection is placed in another plane, another realm of possibility, forming its own shadow circle/triangle, another infinite but bounded set of realizing potentials. The interconnection of the endpoints of these two line bases forms the Platonic solid known as the tetrahedron. This is a triangular pyramid, having a triangular base with lines rising from each point to connect at a position directly above the center of the base. It has four sides, four points, and six edges.

The Primordial Point exists therein as an asymmetric curl, a three dimensional, complex curve with no symmetry to its shape. The extremes of its infinite whirling motions mark out the linear shape of the containing tetrahedron. Just so, the tetrahedron is also created by the intersection of the myriad spherical waves of the two circles/triangles. Rectilinear forms and dimensions can be generated by purely curvilinear interactions. A whole universe of matter, energy, and incarnated consciousness unfolds from the ever complexifying wave interaction/tetrahedral projection. The Qabalah conceives of this secondary creation as a descent through an incalculably vast Abyss, on the other side of which are another seven Sephiroth representing the celestial/conscious worlds and the terrestrial/incarnate world.

Just as the extremes of motion of the asymmetric curl mark out the tetrahedron, so the extremes of motion of the tetrahedron/spherical wave interference pattern extend to the square and the cube. The tetrahedron in motion becomes the pyramid. The materialization of pure information that began as a symmetry break of pure nothingness into a focal point has become the cube of space containing all astral and terrestrial powers, the material world of human experience.

Integration of the four elements in a human being reveals the pyramid, the focused cube, which points the way back to the beginning, through all intervening worlds and states. The process of magick is the process of initiation and the process of creation. The power of all is one, elegantly represented by the pyramid.

It is not surprising, then, if those who work with Enochian magick get visions involving pyramids. More than any other form of subtle force manipulation, Enochian evocation recapitulates the creative and initiatory processes that have brought transcendence and power to magicians of the western mystery tradition. John Dee's Watchtower tablets and his Sigillum Dei Aemeth express the dimensional unfoldment and holographic expansion that mirror the actual cosmic creative processes. These are the very powers which carry the imprint of the magician's Will, that very first cosmic Will of the Primordial Point conditioned by incarnate experience, into the material world.

To ascend the Path of initiation to the top of the magical pyramid is to assimilate the first symmetry break into personal being. The magical summit is realized to be an All-Worlds Point, connecting every state to every other state in the celestial and terrestrial realms. The core source and truth of the magician's personal being is the nexus of all possible and realized worlds.

The magician has brought her/his own creative source into being and so completed a time loop of paradoxical creation. S/He achieves the ultimate realization that the entire universe was created by her/his Will, so eloquently expressed by the great Hermetic dictum, "Deus est Homo." The cause (Deity) is the effect of its own effect. The effect (Humanity) is the cause of its own cause. Time is revealed to be not an arrow but an ocean of waves whose interactions unfold the tetrahedron of celestial space-time and the pyramid of terrestrial unity. Enochian initiation uncovers these mysteries to the diligent and persevering aspirant to truth, unity, and power.

CHAPTER 8
PRACTICE

RITUALS FOR TRAINING AND FOR BUILDING MORE COMPLEX CEREMONIES

The Greater Ritual of the Pentagram

The Greater Ritual of the Hexagram

The Middle Pillar Exercise

Skrying Into The Spirit Vision With The Tattwas

The simple rituals and ceremonial formulae mentioned in the suggested training course can be found in this chapter. The magician is free to make changes to these instructions, use them as blueprints to create new rituals, or replace them outright with ceremonies from other magical traditions. The work of the occultist is to find those symbolic keys and formulae which open her or his mind to the hidden forces of the unconscious and of nature. The only value of any ritual is that it works for the practitioner. What follows is more of the salad bar of ideas for magical training and practice as introduced in the training chapters.

The Greater Ritual Of the Pentagram

ELEMENT	DIRECTION	ELEMENTAL COLOR	COMPLEMENTARY COLOR	GODNAME
Air (Active)	East	Yellow	Violet	IHVH
Fire (Active)	South	Red	Green	ALHIM
Water (Passive)	West	Blue	Orange	AL
Earth (Passive)	North	Black	White	ADNI
Active Spirit	Above/Far East	White	Black	AHIH
Passive Spirit	Above/Far East	Black	White	A.G.L.A.
Spirit	Above/Far East			

The pentagram is used in ceremonial magick to conjure and control the forces of the elements. The lesser form of the pentagram ritual is intended to manipulate the most basic of elemental energies to provide a basic training exercise and everyday personal auric cleansing ceremony. The more advanced, greater form uses the correspondences listed in the above table as general formulae to craft a more specific method of elemental manipulation. The supreme form of the pentagram ritual uses all of these correspondences to call all four elements together as a complete balancing of energies. A pathway to a more transcendent existence may then be opened by this all encompassing confluence. Leaving the terrestrial setting to enter the celestial, astral level of conscious operation enables the adept in magick to perfectly control all elemental energies and spirits from outside of them.

The basic form of the greater pentagram ritual is the same as that of the lesser form: begin with the Qabalistic Cross (a ritualized genuflection), project pentagrams in the four primary directions and charge each with the appropriate Godname, call the four elemental archangels, and end with the Qabalistic Cross. The differences are in the use of color and the incorporation of the spirit pentagrams in the ritual.

The pentagrams of the lesser form are visualized as electric blue with no other background than what is already in the magician's surroundings. The greater form requires visualization of the primary and complementary colors attributed to the elements. The magician visualizes a field of the element's color covering the quarter corresponding to that element. The pentagram itself is drawn in the complementary color.

Such color combinations are known to produce an optical illusion. The colors appear to flash together as their respective light waves interfere with each other. This flashing is to be visualized along with the field and pentagram colors to achieve a maximum of charging of elemental force. The magician can experiment with this phenomenon by placing objects of complementary color next to each other and gazing at them for several minutes. Vibrant colors should flash easily. Red and green flash most prominently together while blue and orange tend to be subtle in their flashing.

The supreme pentagram ritual formula has been used as the basis for many more complicated ceremonies whose purpose is to reach to a higher state of being or to invoke the Higher and Divine Genius, called the Holy Guardian Angel by Aleister Crowley. The ceremonies featured in his *Liber Samekh* and *Liber Reguli* adhere closely to this form. The Golden Dawn also incorporated this ritual pattern in the ceremony of opening the magical temple by the Enochian Watchtowers.

It is necessary for the practitioner of modern western ceremonial magick to be intimately familiar with all the pentagram rituals to be able to recognize their appearance in the literature and to use the ceremonies therein for maximum effect. A host of new rituals can be created based on these basic patterns to work with energies from other traditions which correspond to the five elements. Any work of nature can begin with the G.I.R.P. The invoking form of the lesser pentagram ritual can be done for a quick pick-me-up or as prelude to meditation. Some examples will illustrate how the greater pentagram ritual forms are employed for basic elemental work.

Example 1: The Greater Pentagram Ritual of Fire

Face south, the direction attributed to the active element of Fire, and perform the Qabalistic Cross as given in the Lesser Ritual of the Pentagram.

Visualize a white field, the color of Active Spirit, covering the southern quarter of the magical workplace. Draw with the finger, dagger, or wand the invoking form of the Active Spirit pentagram in black lines, the complementary color of white, against the white background. Imagine the flashing that occurs when black objects are placed in front of a white background. Point to the center of the pentagram and vibrate the Godname, AHIH, pronounced a-hay-yay. Imagine and feel the field and pentagram increase in intensity and emanation of energy.

Visualize a red field, the color of the element of Fire, covering the charged white field and black pentagram. The Active Spirit energies remain present in the background and serve as a balancing and fixing principle for the active elemental Fire powers. Draw the invoking form of the Fire pentagram in green lines, the complementary color of red, against the red background. Imagine the flashing of these two vibrant colors, point to the center of the pentagram, and vibrate the Godname, ALHIM, pronounced as el-o-heem. Imagine and feel the energies of elemental Fire pour into the magical workplace, balanced and ordered by the underlying principle of Active Spirit.

Draw a connecting red line to the west, going clockwise. Project the Active Spirit and Fire pentagrams in the same way as in the south. Repeat for north and east and then close the circle in the south.

Invoke the archangels as given in the Lesser Ritual of the Pentagram but start with Michael. Say, "Before me, Michael. Behind me, Auriel. On my right hand, Gabriel. On my left hand, Raphael. For about me flames the pentagram and in the column shines the six rayed star."

Repeat the Qabalistic Cross to finish the ritual. Proceed with any other Fire work to be done.

Use the banishing forms of the Active Spirit and Fire pentagrams with the above instructions to banish Fire when all other work has been accomplished.

Example 2: The Greater Pentagram Ritual of Water

Face west, the direction attributed to the passive element of Water, and perform the Qabalistic Cross as given in the Lesser Ritual of the Pentagram.

Visualize a black field, the color of Passive Spirit, covering the western quarter of the magical workplace. Draw with the finger, dagger, or wand the invoking form of the Passive Spirit pentagram in white lines, the complementary color of black, against the black background. Imagine the flashing that occurs when white objects are placed in front of a black background. Point to the center of the pentagram and vibrate the Godname, A.G.L.A., which is the anagram, called the notariqon in Qabalah, for Atah Geboor le-Olam Adonai. The magician is advised to actually say the full Godname rather than the anagram, Agla. Imagine and feel the field and pentagram increase in intensity and emanation of energy.

Visualize a blue field, the color of the element of Water, covering the charged black field and white pentagram. The Passive Spirit energies remain present in the background and serve as a balancing and fixing principle for the passive elemental Water powers. Draw the invoking form of the Water pentagram in orange lines, the complementary color of blue, against the blue background. Imagine the subtle flashing of these two colors, point to the center of the pentagram, and vibrate the Godname, AL, pronounced as el. Imagine and feel the energies of elemental Water pour into the magical workplace, balanced and ordered by the underlying principle of Passive Spirit.

Draw a connecting blue line to the north, going clockwise. Project the Passive Spirit and Water pentagrams in the same way as in the west. Repeat for east and south and then close the circle in the west.

Invoke the archangels as given in the Lesser Ritual of the Pentagram but start with Gabriel. Say, "Before me, Gabriel. Behind me, Raphael. On my right hand, Auriel. On my left hand, Michael. For about me flames the pentagram and in the column shines the six rayed star."

Repeat the Qabalistic Cross to finish the ritual. Proceed with any other Water work to be done.

Use the banishing forms of the Passive Spirit and Water pentagrams with the above instructions to banish Water when all other work has been accomplished.

Example 3: The Supreme Ritual of the Pentagram

Face east and perform the Qabalistic cross.

Visualize a white field, the color of Active Spirit, covering the eastern quarter of the magical workplace. Draw with the finger, dagger, or wand the invoking form of the Active Spirit pentagram in black lines, the complementary color of white, against the white background. Imagine the flashing that occurs when black objects are placed in front of a white background. Point to the center of the pentagram and vibrate the Godname, AHIH, pronounced a-hay-yay. Imagine and feel the field and pentagram increase in intensity and emanation of energy.

Visualize a yellow field, the color of the active element of Air, covering the charged white field and black pentagram. The Active Spirit energies remain present in the background and serve as a balancing and fixing principle for the active elemental Air powers. Draw the invoking form of the Air pentagram in violet lines, the complementary color of yellow, against the yellow background. Imagine the flashing of these two vibrant colors, point to the center of the pentagram, and vibrate the Godname, IHVH, pronounced as yod-hay-vav-hay or yah-weh or jehovah. Imagine and feel the energies of elemental Air pour into the magical workplace, balanced and ordered by the underlying principle of Active Spirit.

Draw a connecting line to the south, going clockwise. Project the Active Spirit pentagram as done in the east.

Visualize a red field, the color of the element of Fire, covering the charged white field and black pentagram. Draw the invoking form of the Fire pentagram in green lines, the complementary color of red, against the red background. Imagine the flashing of these two vibrant colors, point to the center of the pentagram, and vibrate the Godname, AL-HIM, pronounced as el-o-heem. Imagine and feel the energies of elemental Fire pour into the magical workplace, balanced and ordered by the underlying principle of Active Spirit.

Draw a connecting line to the west, going clockwise. Project the Passive Spirit pentagram as follows.

Visualize a black field, the color of Passive Spirit, covering the western quarter of the magical workplace. Draw with the finger, dagger, or wand the invoking form of the Passive Spirit pentagram in white lines, the complementary color of black, against the black background. Imagine the flashing that occurs when white objects are placed in front of a black background. Point to the center of the pentagram and vibrate the Godname, A.G.L.A., which is the anagram, called the notariqon in Qabalah, for Atah Geboor le-Olam Adonai. The magician is advised to actually say the full Godname rather than the anagram, Agla. Imagine and feel the field and pentagram increase in intensity and emanation of energy.

Visualize a blue field, the color of the element of Water, covering the charged black field and white pentagram. Draw the invoking form of the Water pentagram in orange lines, the complementary color of blue, against the blue background. Imagine the subtle flashing of these two colors, point to the center of the pentagram, and vibrate the Godname, AL, pronounced as el. Imagine and feel the energies of elemental Water pour into the magical workplace, balanced and ordered by the underlying principle of Passive Spirit.

Draw a connecting line to the north, going clockwise. Project the Passive Spirit pentagram as done in the west.

Visualize a black field, the color of the element of Earth, covering the charged black field and white pentagram. Draw the invoking form of the Earth pentagram in white lines, the complementary color of black, against the black background. Imagine the subtle flashing of these two colors, point to the center of the pentagram, and vibrate the Godname,

ADNI, pronounced as a-don-a-ee. Imagine and feel the energies of elemental Earth pour into the magical workplace, balanced and ordered by the underlying principle of Passive Spirit.

Draw a connecting line to the east, going clockwise. Invoke the archangels as given in the Lesser Ritual of the Pentagram, in that order. Include the sentence about the pentagram and the six rayed star.

Repeat the Qabalistic Cross to finish the ritual. The magician is now surrounded by a balanced, still space in which every elemental force is offset by its complement force. There is great potential but nothing actually emerges. A pathway to a transcendent state of being may be revealed in the subtle tension of balanced energies.

Use the banishing forms of the pentagrams with the above instructions to banish all the elemental forces when the meditation has been completed.

The Greater Ritual Of the Hexagram

Correspondences of the Planets

PLANET	SEPHIRAH	HEXAGRAM POINT	PLANETARY COLOR	COMPLEMENTARY COLOR
Saturn	Binah	Top	Indigo	Amber
Jupiter	Chesed	Upper Right	Violet	Yellow
Mars	Geburah	Upper Left	Red	Green
Sun	Tiphareth	Center	Orange	Blue
Venus	Netzach	Lower Right	Green	Red
Mercury	Hod	Lower Left	Yellow	Violet
Moon	Yesod	Bottom	Blue	Orange

SEPHIRAH	GODNAME	ARCHANGEL	CHOIR OF ANGELS	PALACE OF ASSIAH
Binah	IHVH ALHIM	Tzaphkiel	Aralim	Shabatai (Saturn)
Chesed	AL	Tzadkiel	Chasmalim	Tzedek (Jupiter)
Geburah	ALHIM GEBUR	Kamael	Seraphim	Madim (Mars)
Tiphareth	IHVH ALOAH VA DOTh	Raphael	Melakim	Shemesh (Sun)
Netzach	IHVH TzABAOTh	Haniel	Elohim	Nogah (Venus)
Hod	ALHIM TzABAOTh	Michael	Beni Elohim	Kokab (Mercury)
Yesod	ShADI AL ChAI	Gabriel	Kerubim	Levanah (Moon)

Correspondences of the Zodiacal Signs

ZODIACAL SIGN	RULING PLANET	PLANETARY COLOR	COMPLEMENTARY COLOR
Aries	Mars	Red	Green
Taurus	Venus	Red-Orange	Blue-Green
Gemini	Mercury	Orange	Blue
Cancer	Moon	Orange-Yellow (Amber)	Violet-Blue (Indigo)
Leo	Sun	Yellow	Violet
Virgo	Mercury	Green-Yellow	Red-Violet
Libra	Venus	Green	Red
Scorpio	Mars	Blue-Green	Red-Orange
Saggitarius	Jupiter	Blue	Orange
Capricorn	Saturn	Violet-Blue (Indigo)	Orange-Yellow (Amber)
Aquarius	Saturn	Violet	Yellow
Pisces	Jupiter	Red-Violet	Green-Yellow

ZODIACAL PALACES	RULING ANGEL	ARCHANGEL	GODNAME
Taleh (Aries)	Sharhiel	Malkidiel	ALHIM GEBUR
Shor (Taurus)	Araziel	Asmodel	IHVH TzABAOTh
Teomim (Gemini)	Sarayel	Ambriel	ALHIM TzABAOTh
Sarton (Cancer)	Pakiel	Muriel	ShADI AL ChAI
Ariah (Leo)	Sharatiel	Verkiel	IHVH ALOAH VA DOTh
Betulah (Virgo)	Shelatiel	Damaliel	ALHIM TzABAOTh
Moznaim (Libra)	Chedeqiel	Zuriel	IHVH TzABAOTh
Aqrab (Scorpio)	Saitziel	Barkiel	ALHIM GEBUR
Qesheth (Saggitarius)	Saritiel	Advakiel	AL
Gedi (Capricorn)	Samaqiel	Hanael	IHVH ALHIM
Deli (Aquarius)	Zakmaqiel	Cambriel	IHVH ALHIM
Dagim (Pisces)	Vakabiel	Amnitziel	AL

The hexagram is used in ceremonial magick to conjure and control the forces of the planets and zodiacal signs. The lesser form of the hexagram ritual is used to generate and purge basic celestial energy in preparation for further planetary or zodiacal work. The more advanced, greater form uses the correspondences in the above tables as general formulae to craft a more specific method of manipulation of celestial powers. The adept has left the terrestrial realm of the elements to commune with the cosmic streams of impersonal consciousness through the use of the magical hexagram.

Both the lesser and greater forms of the hexagram ritual begin with the keyword analysis. Golden Dawn orders typically use the Christian mystical formula of INRI, thought to top the cross to which Christ was nailed at his crucifixion, and symbolically transform this into the name of the Gnostic high God, IAO. The Golden Dawn adept initiation ceremony, the introduction into their inner order of Rosea Rubea et Aurea Crucis, is developed according to this formula.

An alternative keyword analysis and formula, based on Thelemic ideals, can be found in an appendix to the book, *Enochian Initiation* by Frater W.I.T. This formula transforms the name of the Thelemic deific ideal, HERU, into the supreme word of Thelemic magick, ABRAHADABRA. A discussion of its symbolism and underlying principles of new aeon advanced initiation may also be found therein. The adept may choose either of these or develop her or his own personal initiatory formula.

The cosmic forces represented by the hexagram may be channeled and manipulated by the duly initiated adept of Hermetic magick, whose formula of spiritual transcendence has been brought to bear in the magical workplace. The ritual is performed while facing east, the place of dawn, the brilliant realization of the sun emerging from the darkness of night. This is the ideal metaphor for spiritual realization used in magical and religious traditions throughout all times and places. The psychological term, the solar-phallus, refers to this state of being and becoming.

The Golden Dawn magical system specifies four different, "elemental" forms of the hexagram, one of which is the familiar upright and inverted interlaced triangles, to be used in the lesser form of the hexagram ritual. However, the Star of David form may be employed in all four quarters to simplify performance.

The adept visualizes a white field covering the eastern section of the magical workplace and then traces the hexagram with the finger or wand, imagined in gold lines, onto this field. The Saturn hexagram may be used in the east, south, west, and north quarters, respectively.

In each case, the adept points to the center of the golden star and vibrates the notariqon,

A.R.A.R.I.T.A., which stands for "Achud Rash Achudotho Rash Yechudotho Temoratho Achud." It means, "One is His beginning. One is His individuality. His permutation one." Qabalists use this statement to affirm the unity of their God. The ultimate nature of all cosmic scale energies is hereby identified with the supreme creator of all existence, from the greatest to the least.

The ritual is ended with the keyword analysis which began the proceeding in order to incorporate the newly projected energies into the transcendent state of the adept. Further planetary or zodiacal work or general meditation on the celestial realm may be done thereafter.

The greater form of the hexagram ritual uses the colors and deific hierarchy of a particular planet or sign to invoke or banish that power. Each planet has its own hexagram, drawn by starting at the point attributed to it. The general rule is to trace clockwise to invoke and counterclockwise to banish. For example, to draw the Saturn hexagram, start at the top point and draw downward to the right, over to the left, and back to the top. Trace the inverted triangle to complete the figure by starting from the bottom point, opposite to the top, and draw upward to the left, over to the right, and back to the bottom. The second triangle should be superimposed on the first to establish the form of the hexagram. Visualize this figure as made up of amber lines drawn on an indigo field, according to the above table of correspondences. The Godname, the archangel name, and A.R.A.R.I.T.A. are used to charge the hexagram in each of the four quarters of the magical workplace.

The major difference between the lesser and greater forms of this ritual is the use of a fifth hexagram, drawn after the circle of colors, hexagrams, and magical names is completed. Once the workplace is saturated with the colors and powers of the planet being worked, the adept turns clockwise until she or he faces the approximate direction of where the actual planet is in the sky at the time of the ritual. This may be calculated using an ephemeris or an astrology application on a computer. Use this reference to determine which zodiacal signs the sun and the target planet are in. Locate the approximate position of the sun in the sky at the time of the ritual. That is about where the sign that the sun is in is located. Imagine the wheel of the zodiac surrounding the magical workplace to locate the sign the target planet. Use the entire deific hierarchy as well as A.R.A.R.I.T.A. to charge the fifth hexagram. The planetary energies should pour from this figure like water from a fire hose at full blast. Complete the circle to face east and finish with the keyword analysis.

As is evident from the above table of planetary correspondences, the usage of the hexagram for the sun is an anomaly. This is attributed to the center of the hexagram rather than a specific point. The Golden Dawn magical system specifies that all the other planetary hexagrams should be used, one at a time, for each quarter. This is tiresome and taxing on the concentration as all the colors and their complements would be involved. Aleister Crowley recommended the use of the unicursal hexagram for solar hexagram rituals.

Zodiacal sign invocations work the same way as the planetary rituals. They have their own colors, archangels, angels, and cosmic palaces (spheres of influence). The hexagram and Godname of the ruling planet should be used. Consult the above tables of zodiacal correspondences for the details of each sign. Otherwise, the ritual form is the same. Some examples will clarify these ceremonies.

Example 1: The Greater Hexagram Ritual of Jupiter

Determine the approximate position of Jupiter in the sky at the time of the ritual performance using an ephemeris or an astrology application. This will be the position of the fifth hexagram to be drawn at the edge of the circle.

Face east and perform the keyword analysis. Realize the full impact of whatever initiation or higher ideal this expresses.

Visualize a violet field covering the eastern quarter. Draw the invoking Jupiter hexagram in yellow lines with the finger or wand. Start at the upper right point and trace downward and to the left to reach the bottom point of an inverted triangle. Continue upwards to the left and then over to the right to complete the triangle. Move to the lower left point and trace the upright triangle. Draw upwards to the right, crossing the inverted triangle already traced, to reach the top point of the figure. Continue downwards to the right and then over to the left to complete the upright triangle and so the whole hexagram.

Visualize the flashing of the violet field and yellow figure. Point to the center of the hexagram and vibrate the Godname, AL, the archangel name, Tzadkiel, and A.R.A.R.I.T.A.

Draw a connecting violet line to the south, moving clockwise, and project another Jupiter hexagram as was done in the east. Repeat for west and north and then complete the circle by moving back to the east.

Go to the edge of the circle in the east and walk clockwise or turn clockwise from the center to face the approximate position of Jupiter. Draw the fifth hexagram as done in the quarters in the direction of the planet. Point to the center and vibrate the God-name, AL, the archangel name, Tzadkiel, the name of the angelic choir, Chasmalim, the Jupiterian Palace of Assiah, Tzedek, and A.R.A.R.I.T.A. The adept may want to utter the full sentence, Achud Rash Achudotho Rash Yechudotho Temoratho Achud, at this point in the ritual instead of its notariqon.

Feel a flood of Jupiterian force flow into the magical workplace from this specially placed hexagram. The adept will have succeeded in invoking power from the most sublime expression of Jupiter in the Qabalistic world of Atziluth, through the archangelic world of Briah, through the angelic world of Yetzirah, and into the sphere of Jupiter in Assiah. The magical workplace will have become a focal point of this palace in the material world, capable of manifesting the energies excited by the cross planar stream.

Return to the east and, if necessary, to the center, and repeat the keyword analysis. Proceed with whatever meditations or magical operations are intended to utilize the Jupiterian energy. Repeat this ritual using the banishing Jupiter hexagram before closing.

Example 2: The Greater Hexagram Ritual of Taurus

Determine the approximate position of Taurus in the sky at the time of the ritual performance using an ephemeris or an astrology application. This will be the position of the fifth hexagram to be drawn at the edge of the circle.

Face east and perform the keyword analysis. Realize the full impact of whatever initiation or higher ideal this expresses.

Visualize a red-orange field covering the eastern quarter. The planet Venus rules Taurus so trace the hexagram starting at the Venus point, lower right. Draw a blue-green line to the left, then upwards to the right, and then downwards to the right to complete the upright triangle. Move to the upper left point and draw the overlapping inverted triangle by tracing to the right, downwards to the left, and then upwards to the left to complete the hexagram.

Visualize the flashing of colors with their astral vibrations. Point to the center of the hexagram and vibrate the Godname, IHVH TzABAOTh, the archangel name, Asmodel, and A.R.A.R.I.T.A.

Draw a connecting red-orange line to the south, moving clockwise, and project another Taurus hexagram as was done in the east. Repeat for west and north and then complete the circle by moving back to the east.

Go to the edge of the circle in the east and walk clockwise or turn clockwise from the center to face the approximate position of Taurus. Draw the fifth hexagram as done in the quarters in the direction of the planet. Point to the center and vibrate the God-name, IHVH TzABAOTh, the archangel, Asmodel, the name of the ruling angel, Araziel, the Palace of Assiah of Taurus, Shor, and A.R.A.R.I.T.A. The adept may want to utter the full sentence, Achud Rash Achudotho Rash Yechudotho Temoratho Achud, at this point in the ritual instead of its no-tariqon.

Return to the east and, if necessary, to the center, and repeat the keyword analysis. Proceed with whatever meditations or magical operations are intended to utilize the energy of Taurus. Repeat this ritual using the banishing Taurus hexagram before closing.

The Middle Pillar Exercise

The purpose of The Middle Pillar Exercise is to establish a column of energy down the center of the body and circulate this accelerated power throughout the aura. Five globes of shining color are visualized along a line from the top of the head to the bottoms of the feet. They correspond to the Sephiroth on the Middle Pillar of the Tree of Life: Kether, the Crown; the unnumbered Sephirah named Daath, meaning Knowledge; Tiphareth, meaning Beauty; Yesod, meaning the Foundation; and Malkuth, meaning the Kingdom.

The colors corresponding to these spheres of creative process are brilliant white, grayish white, yellow, violet, and dark olive-green. A white line is visualized as connecting these spheres to give the pillar of creative force a continuity of flow. The power is circulated around the periphery of the body with specific patterns of visualization to accelerate the entire aura. This process is useful for general magical training and as a preliminary to other occult works.

The five globes roughly correspond to five of the seven primary chakras of Hindu lore: the crown sphere to Sahasrara, the neck sphere to Visuddha, the heart sphere to Anahatta, the genital sphere to Svadhisthana, and the sphere at the feet to Muladhara. However, the colors of the globes are different from those usually attributed to the chakras and two of the auric centers, Ajna and Manipura, are left out. The colors of the seven planets are usually attributed to the chakras in the western magical tradition. Several different schemes may be found in the various books on this subject but the most prevalent system is that used by the Hermetic Order of the Golden Dawn. Starting from the crown of the head, the attributions are yellow for Mercury, violet for Luna, green for Venus, orange for Sol, blue for Jupiter, red for Mars, and the four colors of Malkuth: citrine, olive, russet, and black, for Saturn.

Thus, it may be understood that the Middle Pillar Exercise is not intended as a western style Kundalini Yoga, especially since the energy is initially developed downwards. This is not to say that Kundalini effects can never result from continued practice of this exercise. Any auric manipulation work can eventually achieve them. However, the intent here is to quicken and integrate the aura as a whole to promote efficient channeling of cosmic forces generated by subsequent magical practice.

1. Stand erect while facing east.
2. Visualize a globe of brilliant white light above your head, its bottom point touching the top of your head. Vibrate the divine Name AHIH three times, pronounced as Ehayay.
3. Visualize a shaft of brilliant white light move downward from the crown sphere, through your head, to your neck. Visualize a

globe of grayish white light there and vibrate the divine Name IHVH ALHIM three times, pronounced as Yahweh Elohim.

4. Continue the shaft of white light downward to the center of your chest and visualize a globe of golden yellow light there. Vibrate the divine Name IHVH ALVH VDOT three times, pronounced as Yahweh Eloah Va Dot.

5. Continue the shaft of white light downward to a point two inches below your navel and visualize a globe of violet light there. Vibrate the divine Name ShDI AL ChAI three times, pronounced as Shaddaiee El Chaiee.

6. Continue the shaft of white light downward to a point between your feet. Visualize a globe of dark olive-green light there, half above the floor of the temple and half below. Vibrate the divine Name ADNI HARTz three times, pronounced as Adonaiee Ha Aretz.

7. Reinforce the visualization of all five colored globes with the connecting shaft of white light and feel the integration of all the energy in your physical and Light bodies. Start a current of energy moving from the top of your head down the front of your body to your feet and then back to the top of your head from behind. Send energy down the right side of your body, around your feet, and then up the left. Raise a stream of energy from your feet up the central shaft of visualization to your head and then out the

top in a shower of sparks that fall all around your body. Finally, feel all the energies and currents of your physical and Light bodies reach out to the farthest stars to establish a universal connection. You are now ready to do magick as a complete microcosm, a true mirror of all that was, is, and shall be.

Skrying Into the Spirit Vision With the Tattwas

TATTWA	ELEMENT	SHAPE	PRIMARY COLOR	COMPLIMENTARY COLOR
Akasha	Spirit	Oval	Black	White
Tejas	Fire	Triangle	Red	Green
Apas	Water	Crescent	Silver	Maroon
Vayu	Air	Disk	Blue	Orange
Prithivi	Earth	Square	Yellow	Violet

The five tattwas of Hindu magick correspond to the five elements of the western magical tradition. They are represented by five colored shapes that can be used as focuses of meditation and what the magicians of the Golden Dawn called skrying into the spirit vision. To skry is to gaze deeply into an object such as a crystal ball, a dark mirror, or any colored stone for the purposes of learning hidden information from knowledgeable spirits. The Hindu tattwas can be used as keys into the greatest magick mirror of all, the human imagination. The hidden realms of the mind may be plumbed for knowledge of the significance of the elements. The wider astral plane may be reached with enough practice in skrying.

The five tattwas consist of a red triangle for Fire, called Tejas, a silver crescent for Water, called Apas, a blue disk for Air, called Vayu, a yellow square for Earth, called Prithivi, and a black oval for Spirit, called Akasha. These colors are not all the same as those used in the western tradition. It is important for the magician to keep in mind which system she or he is using and for what purpose. However, the adepts of the Golden Dawn found tattwa skrying to be very useful in developing the inner senses and as a preparation for more advanced magick. Skrying into the spirit vision is a worthwhile preliminary for astral travel, that is, travelling through the myriad planes of existence in the Body of Light. This involves an out of body experience while skrying involves an exploration of the imagination with the magician firmly seated within the body.

The process of tattwa skrying involves looking at one of the five images, drawn on a card or cut out of construction paper, until you see an after image in the complimentary color. This after image is then taken into imagination and used as a seed for a visionary experience involving the related element. Not only does this process open and expand the imagination but is instructive as to how the element operates in the various states of nature. Such knowledge is vital for any subsequent alchemical work.

There are twenty-five subtattwas, just as there are twenty-five subelements. Examples of these are Prithivi of Vayu – Earth of Air and Tejas of Akasha – Fire of Spirit. The theory behind these is that each element has five different manifestations corresponding to the influence of each of the elements within that element. For instance, Earth of Air refers to the most dense and material manifestation of Air. Fire of Spirit refers to the most active and powerful expressions of Spirit. This scheme hold true for the subangles of the Enochian elemental tablets. The various angels and spirits residing in those areas of the Watchtowers of John Dee express their subelement according to their specific natures.

The images of the subtattwas are made by placing a small tattwa image inside a larger tattwa image. Naturally, a native subelement such as Fire of Fire or Water of Water would be no different than the element itself. For example, the subtattwa image for Vayu of Tejas consists of a small blue disk placed inside a large red triangle. Its complimentary image will be a small yellow disk inside a large green triangle.

Here are the instructions to perform a tattwa skrying:

1. Perform a basic banishing ritual such as the Lesser Banishing Pentagram Ritual.
2. Perform a Greater Invoking Pentagram Ritual for the element of the tattwa to be skryed or the main element of the subtattwa to be skryed. For example, the main element of Prithivi of Apas, Earth of Water, is Water. Earth is the subelement, that particular aspect of Water. In this case, use the Water pentagram ritual.
3. Place the tattwa image before you and gaze at it until you see a shimmering effect. Look away from the image onto a white surface such as a wall and see the complimentary af-

ter image. Perform this several times to fix these images in your mind.

4. Perform the systematic body relaxation and rhythmic breathing exercise given in Track 1 of the training program in this book.

5. Enter into meditation and visualize the primary image of the tattwa on a door. Then, visualize the after image appear on the door to replace the primary image. Mentally open the door and see with your mind's eye what is beyond. Move through the door and journey through the landscapes and other visions that appear.

6. When you're ready to return to normal waking consciousness, visualize the door you came through and move yourself back through it. Close the door, change the after image back to the primary image, and then focus your awareness to your physical surroundings.

7. Record in as much detail as possible all of your visionary experiences in your magical diary. Include any relevant insights, associations and memories you may have gained.

8. Banish whatever element you invoked with the appropriate Greater Banishing Pentagram Ritual. It is best to use the specific banishing form rather than the general, lesser banishing form when you invoke a particular magical energy.

The scheme of the elements and subelements becomes clearer over time. A great deal of understanding of nature in its relations to the occult forces may be developed with much practice. Oracles of various sorts may be created using this method of skrying.

CHAPTER 9
PRACTICE

ADVANCED ENOCHIAN MAGICAL CEREMONIES

Evocation of the Four Seniors of a Particular
Plant or the Four Kings Together –
Full Temple Ceremony

Evocation of the Four Seniors of a Particular
Plant or the Four Kings Together –
Short Form Ceremony

Evocation of the Several Types of Subangle
Angels – Full Temple Ceremony

All Elementals Evocation Ceremony

Evocation of the Thirty Aethyrs

The Enochian magical ceremonies in this chapter
build on those given in *Enochian Initiation*. It will
help the reader to be familiar with the practices de-

tailed in the appendices of this book to understand what is being done in the ceremonies herein. They will take the practitioner to a new height of power and understanding of the Enochian universe. Influence over the material world will build from this foundation. Experience in this work will constitute the operator as an adept.

Evocation of the Four Seniors of a Particular Planet or the Four Kings Together – Full Temple Ceremony

Temple Setup:

Set up a double cubed Altar in the middle of a square or rectangular room. Place a pedestal in the center of each wall, marking out the four quarters of existence. Each direction is infinite and reaches into a higher than physical world. The reaches of infinity focus on the central altar from the east, south, west, north, above, and below. Thus, the altar is the center of the universe, the point of balance from which any energy may be launched to cause any effect anywhere.

Each pedestal marks the nature of its quarter, indicating the frequency of magical power emanating from that particular infinity. These four currents are symbolized by the four elements of classical Greek science: Air, Fire, Water, and Earth. Mark the nature of Air in the east by placing an emblem of that which rules the airy nature such as the Angelic Air Tablet. Place a white votive candle in front of the tablet to light the darkling, mysterious abyss of the east. Place an emblem of the element itself with the candle, such as a hand fan or rose. Place the Angelic Spirit Tablet, called the Tablet of Union, in the far east raised above the other tablets.

In the south, place the symbols of Fire: the Angelic Fire Tablet, a white votive, and a red lamp, red candle, or candle in a red holder. In the west, place the symbols of Water: the Angelic Water Tablet, a white votive, and a cup or bowl of pure water. In the north, place the symbols of Earth: the Angelic Earth Tablet, a white votive, and a plate of salt.

Let the Altar, symbolizing the consciousness of the magician, center of his/her universe, be covered with a black cloth draping down on all sides to touch the floor or painted black. Place the four elemental weapons on top of the Altar, answering to the elemental natures of the quarters. Thus, place the Air Dagger on the eastern side of the altar, place the Fire Wand on the southern side, place the Water Cup on the western side, and place the Earth Pentacle on the northern side. In the center, the center of All, place a flask of fragrant Oil, symbolizing the ubiquitous element of Spirit. Oil of cinnamon or Abramelin oil are appropriate. A favored Holy Book may be placed underneath the flask if desired. In this way, the magician is expressed as a microcosm, an entire universe in miniature, whose several natures correspond to the forces of creation.

Place a Censor on the southern side of the Altar or the southern pedestal as desired, burning frankincense and myrrh or incense of Abramelin. Place the Bell at any convenient spot. Embellish the Altar with crystals, black, white, or multicolored tapers, etc.

Prepare the water in the Cup on the altar by dropping a few particles of salt into it and say, "May the salt of Earth admonish the Waters to bear the virtue of the Great Sea."

Astral Temple Visualization and Auric Preparation:

Take three deep breaths to calm your mood and focus your attention. Close your eyes and visualize your body of light detach from your physical body and begin to rise upward. Reach the ceiling of your physical temple and then move through this. Continue rising above your building, high into the air at ever increasing speed. See the clouds fly by you as your energy body reaches beyond the earth's atmosphere.

Launch yourself with a great burst of acceleration into outer space, leaving the entire planet earth far behind. The sun becomes just a point of light in the midst of the darkness of the void, one among myriad others. Travel lightyears in seconds with the speed of thought as you finally reach the cosmic temple, set amidst the vastness of deep space. It is in the shape of a torus, like a huge donut. Each wheel of that greater wheel is a flow of brilliant white light. A current of blue power flows through the middle of all these wheels on the same plane as the torus as a whole. All the furniture and implements of the physical temple are placed in the central space surrounded by the wheel of wheels with the altar in the center of all. A spike of downward shooting brilliant white light passes through the middle of the altar, an axle of the wheel.

Move your body of light to the west side of the astral altar, facing the east of the temple and perform a Middle Pillar Exercise or a Rousing of the Citadels ritual. Visualize a ball of brilliant white light above your head, its bottom point touching the top of your head. Vibrate the divine Name AHIH three times, pronounced as Ehayay.

Send a shaft of brilliant white light downward from the crown sphere, through your head, to your neck. Visualize a grayish white ball of light there and vibrate the divine Name IHVH ALHIM three times, pronounced as Yahweh Elohim.

Continue the shaft of light downward to the center of your chest and visualize a golden yellow ball there. Vibrate the divine Name IHVH ALVH VDOT three times, pronounced as Yahweh Eloah Va Dot.

Continue the shaft of light downward to a point two inches below your navel and visualize a violet ball of light there. Vibrate the divine Name ShDI AL ChAI three times, pronounced as Shaddaiee El Chaiee.

Continue the shaft of light downward to a point between your feet. Visualize an olive green ball there, half above the floor of the temple and half below. Vibrate the divine Name ADNI HARTz three times, pronounced as Adonaiee Ha Aretz.

Reinforce the visualization of all five colored balls with the connecting shaft of light and feel the integration of all the energy in your physical and light bodies. Start a current of energy moving from the top of your head down the front of your body to your feet and then back to the top of your head from behind. Send energy down the right side of your body and then up the left. Raise a stream of energy from your feet up the central shaft of visualization to your head and then out the top in a shower of sparks that fall all around your body. Finally, feel all the energies and currents of your physical and light bodies reach out to the farthest stars to establish a universal connection. You are now ready to do magick as a complete microcosm, a true mirror of all that was, is, and shall be.

Opening:

Stand on the west side of the Altar, facing east. Perform the Lesser Banishing Ritual of the Pentagram.

Purify the Temple by taking the Cup, moving to the east wall, raising the Cup on high, and saying, "For pure will, unassuaged of purpose, delivered from the lust of result, is every way perfect." (Liber Legis, Chapter 1, Verse 44)

Bring the Cup to heart level and say, "By the Lustral Water of the Loud Resounding Sea, I purify this Temple and all objects and persons within." Mark the points of an inverse triangle with the Cup, upper left, upper right, then lower center. Imagine a blue triangle hanging in midair.

Walk deosil to the south quarter and repeat the above paragraph. Repeat for west and north, return to the east, and walk back to the west side of the Altar in a deosil curve.

Consecrate the Temple by taking up the fuming Censor, moving to the east wall, raising the Censor on high, and saying, "So that thy light is in me; & its red flame is as a sword in my hand to push thy order." (Liber Legis, Chapter 3, Verse 38)

Bring the Censor to heart level and say, "With the Sacred Fire which darts and flashes through the hidden depths of the universe, I consecrate this Temple and all objects and persons within." Mark the points of an upright triangle by swinging the Censor toward the upper center, lower left, then lower right. Ideally, a puff of smoke should be left when the Censor swings away from the point. Imagine a red triangle superimposed on the blue triangle, making a hexagram.

Walk deosil to the south quarter and repeat the above paragraph. Repeat for west and north, return to the east, and walk back to the west side of the altar in a deosil curve. Replace the Censor and take up the Wand.

Open each of the Angelic Tablets in turn, from east through south, west, and north as follows. Stand before the eastern tablet with Wand in hand. Say, "Let us evoke the Powers of Air with the Great Eastern Quadrangle."

Draw the invoking active Spirit pentagram in black against a white background over the tablet, point to the center, and vibrate AHIH and then EXARP. Draw the invoking Air pentagram in violet against a yellow background, vibrating IHVH. Put down the Wand, take up the Fan, and draw the Kerubic sign of Aquarius in violet within the Air pentagram, creating a wind with the Fan. Vibrate Raphael and visualize Him standing behind the tablet.

Replace the Fan, take up the Wand, and draw a golden cross over the Great Cross of the tablet from top to bottom and then left to right. Draw a deosil golden circle around the cross starting from the top point. Point to the center of the cross and say, "In the names and letters of the Great Eastern Quadrangle, I call forth the Powers of Air."

Hold the Wand on high and say, "In the Three Great Secret Names that are borne upon the Banners of the East, (trace the letters of the horizontal line of the Great Cross with the Wand as each Name is vibrated) ORO IBAH AOZPI, I call forth the Powers of Air."

Hold the Wand on high and say, "In the Name of (trace the letters spiraling out from the center) BATAIVAH, great King of the East, I call forth the Powers of Air. Knock.

Go to the southern tablet with Wand in hand. Say, "Let us evoke the Powers of Fire with the Great Southern Quadrangle."

Draw the invoking active Spirit pentagram in black against a white background over the tablet, point to the center, and vibrate AHIH and then BITOM. Draw the invoking Fire pentagram in green against a red background, vibrating ALHIM. Put down the Wand, take up the Red Lamp, and draw the Kerubic sign of Leo in green within the Fire pentagram. Vibrate Michael and visualize Him standing behind the tablet.

Replace the Lamp, take up the Wand, and draw a golden cross over the Great Cross of the tablet from top to bottom and then left to right. Draw a deosil golden circle around the cross. Point to the center of the cross and say, "In the names and letters of the Great Southern Quadrangle, I call forth the Powers of Fire."

Hold the Wand on high and say, "In the Three Great Secret Names that are borne upon the Banners of the South, (trace the letters of the horizontal line of the Great Cross with the wand as each Name is vibrated) OIP TEAA PDOCE, I call forth the Powers of Fire."

Hold the Wand on high and say, "In the Name of (trace the letters spiraling out from the center) EDLPRNAA, great King of the South, I call forth the Powers of Fire." Knock.

Go to the western tablet with Wand in hand. Say, "Let us evoke the Powers of Water with the Great Western Quadrangle."

Draw the invoking passive Spirit pentagram in white against a black background over the tablet, point to the center, and vibrate Atah Geboor Leolahm Adonai and then HCOMA. Draw the invoking Water pentagram in orange against a blue background, vibrating AL. Put down the Wand, take up the Cup, and draw the Kerubic sign of Scorpio in orange within the Water pentagram. Vibrate Gabriel and visualize Him standing behind the tablet.

Replace the Cup, take up the Wand, and draw a golden cross over the Great Cross of the tablet from top to bottom and then left to right. Draw a deosil golden circle around the cross. Point to the center of the cross and say, "In the names and letters of the Great Western Quadrangle, I call forth the Powers of Water."

Hold the Wand on high and say, "In the Three Great Secret Names that are borne upon the Banners of the West, (trace the letters of the horizontal line of the Great Cross with the Wand as each Name is vibrated) MPH ARSL GAIOL, I call forth the Powers of Water."

Hold the Wand on high and say, "In the Name of (trace the letters spiraling out from the center) RAAGIOSL, great King of the West, I call forth the Powers of Water." Knock.

Go to the northern tablet with Wand in hand. Say, "Let us evoke the Powers of Earth with the Great Northern Quadrangle."

Draw the invoking passive Spirit pentagram in white against a black background over the tablet, point to the center, and vibrate Atah Geboor Leolahm Adonai and then NANTA. Draw the invoking Earth pentagram in white against a black background, vibrating ADNI. Put down the Wand, take up the Pentacle, and draw the Kerubic sign of Taurus in white within the Earth pentagram. Vibrate Auriel and visualize Him standing behind the tablet.

Replace the Pentacle, take up the Wand, and draw a golden cross over the Great Cross of the tablet from top to bottom and then left to right. Draw a deosil golden circle around the cross. Point to the center of the cross and say, "In the names and letters of the Great Northern Quadrangle, I call forth the Powers of Earth."

Hold the Wand on high and say, "In the Three Great Secret Names that are borne upon the Banners of the North, (trace the letters of the horizontal line of the Great Cross with the wand as each Name is vibrated) MOR DIAL HCTGA, I call forth the Powers of Earth."

Hold the Wand on high and say, "In the Name of (trace the letters spiraling out from the center) ICZHIHAL, great King of the North, I call forth the Powers of Earth." Knock.

Complete the circle and return to the west side of the Altar, facing east. Say, "Let us evoke the Powers of Spirit with the Tablet of Union."

Draw the invoking active Spirit pentagram in black against a white background and vibrate AHIH. Draw the invoking passive Spirit pentagram in white against a black background over the Tablet of Union, point to the center, and vibrate Atah Geboor Leolahm Adonai. Vibrate EXARP HCOMA NANTA BITOM, tracing the letters with the Wand, starting from the upper left letter and moving downward, one line per Name. Say, "In the Names and Letters of the Tablet of Union, I call forth the Powers of Spirit." Ring 2-1-2 with the Bell.

Intone the first Enochian call: "Ol sonf vorz jee, goho Yad Balt, lonsh kalz vonfo; Sobra zol ror ee ta naz-psad, grah ta mal-perj; dee-es holk kwah no-thoa zimz, od ko-ma ta nob-loh zeen; So-ba theel jeh-nomp perj aldee; Dee-es urbz o-bo-le jee re-sam; Kasarm o-ho-re-la taba Pire; Dee-es zon-renj kab erm yad-na. Pee-la far-zm znurza adna go-no Yad-peel, dee-es hom-to; So-ba eepam, loo eepa-mis; Dee-es lo-ho-lo vep zomd poamal, od bog-pa a-ee ta pee-ap pee-ah-mol od voh-an. Za-ka-re, ka, od zamran; o-do see-kle kwah; zorj, lap zirdo no-ko Mad, ho-ath Yai-da."

Raise the Wand on high and say, "Ye I evoke, oh Angels of the Celestial Spheres. Ye are the Guardi-ans of the Gates of the Universe and of this Magick Sphere. Be here present to shine your transcendent Light on this Cosmic Temple and all within. Achud Rash Achudotho Rash Yechudotho Temoratho Achud." Ring 3-1-3 with the Bell.

Go to the east and face south. Perform the Magick Circumambulation by giving the Sign of the Enterer and then walking around the Temple deosil three times, giving the Sign of the Enterer on passing the east each time. Imagine a current of white light passing through you each time this Sign is given. After three complete turns, return to the west side of the Altar in a deosil curve. A continuously flowing cylinder of subtle white force should have developed around the Temple.

Pronounce the Thelemic Declaration to dedicate every erg of magical energy generated in Temple to the Great Work of realizing the highest levels of consciousness in physical incarnation.

"Holy and Blessed art Thou, Oh Heru Ra Ha, Transcendent Glory that surpasses all things. May Your Infinite Love reach down to bless this temple, dedicated to Your service. Enlighten my mind and enliven my soul so that I may be better enabled to carry out Your Will, which is my Will, here on earth.

Thereby, let the Word of the New Law be pronounced once more so that the brilliant stellar consciousness may be further established in the soul of humanity.

Do what thou wilt shall be the whole of the law. I declare that the purposes and operations of this temple are dedicated to spreading the Law of Thelema throughout the world on all planes to further the evolution of life everywhere. Let this new Covenant, the Third Dispensation of humanity's transcendence, the fulfillment of all previous Laws, be realized in the Collective Consciousness for the healing of all races. Our individual Paths through infinite space are our personal Covenants with the Divine. So may we all come at length to full Self actualization. Love is the law, love under will."

Complete the opening by ringing a battery of 3-5-3 with the Bell, making eleven rings in total, and then make a statement of intent, declaring the purpose and intention of the Rite.

Evocation:

Perform the Lesser Invoking Ritual of the Hexagram with Thelemic Keyword Analysis, beginning with the declaration: "Let the energies of the temple be raised to celestial intensity with Ritual of the Hexagram."

Declare, "Let the four Seniors of <planet> be evoked in due form." Or declare, "Let the four Kings be evoked in due form." Walk to the East with wand in hand and then proceed around the temple to the Earth tablet. Point with the wand to the center and intone the fifth Enochian call of Earth to open the Watchtower.

Conjure the Earth Senior or King by pointing with the wand at the first letter of the name and then trace and intone the name as many times as the number of the Sephirah to which its planet is attributed. For instance, if the Venus Senior is to be evoked, trace and intone its name seven times, since the planet Venus is attributed to the seventh Sephirah, Netzach. Four repetitions would be traced and intoned for the Jupiter Senior, since Jupiter is attributed to Chesed, the fourth Sephirah. The Kings are attributed to Sol and Tiphareth and so six repetitions would be traced and intoned.

Command the angel to stay in place at the Earth tablet and walk around the temple to the east. Open the eastern quadrangle and summon the Air Senior or King with the Air call and trace the name accordingly. Repeat for the Water and Fire angels and then return to the east. Return to the west side of the altar, facing east.

Declare, "I shall now commune with the angels thus evoked." Sit in a comfortable position, relax the body from head to toe, perform some rhythmic breathing, and then open the mind's eye to receive the vision and power of the conjured angels. When you're satisfied with the results of the contact, exit the vision and return to body consciousness. Go to the west side of the altar and face East.

Take up the wand and banish the angels by declaring, "I hereby give <angel names> license to depart. Return unto your habitations and abodes. Let there ever be peace between you and I and be ready to come again when called. For now, depart!" Give one sharp rap on the altar with the wand. Proceed to the closing.

Example: evoking the four Mercury Seniors

Open your magical temple as specified above. Go to the east and walk around the temple to the north. Intone the fifth Enochian call of Earth and then evoke the Mercury Senior of Earth, AHMLICV. This name is traced along the lower left bar of the Great Central Cross eight times, since Mercury is attributed to Hod, the eighth Sephirah.

Walk to the east and intone the third Enochian call of Air. Evoke the Mercury Senior of Air, AVTO-TAR. Continue around the temple to the west and intone the fourth Enochian call of Water. Evoke the Mercury Senior of Water, SONIZNT. Continue around the temple to the south and intone the sixth Enochian call of Fire. Evoke the Mercury Senior of Fire, ANODOIN. Continue around the temple to the east and then return to the west side of the altar, facing east.

Declare, "I shall now commune with the angels thus evoked." Take a seat in a convenient spot and receive the communion of all four Seniors, singly and together. Give them license to depart when satisfied and close the temple in due form.

Closing:

Perform the Lesser Banishing Ritual of the Hexagram with Thelemic Keyword Analysis. Perform the purification and consecration as in the opening. Close the Angelic Tablets as follows:

Go to the eastern tablet, Wand in hand, and say, "Let us banish the Powers of Air with the Great Eastern Quadrangle." Draw the banishing active Spirit pentagram in black against a white background over the tablet, point to the center, and vibrate AHIH and EXARP. Draw the banishing Air pentagram in violet against a yellow background and vibrate IHVH. Draw the Kerubic sign of Aquarius with the Wand in violet within the Air pentagram and vibrate Raphael. Draw a golden cross over the Great Cross of the tablet from top to bottom and then left to right. Draw a widdershins golden circle around the cross. Point to the center and say, "In the names and letters of the Great Eastern Quadrangle, I banish the Powers of Air." Knock once with the Wand.

Repeat appropriate banishing formulas for the other tablets in the south, west, and north. Complete the circle and return to the west side of the Altar, facing east. Say, "Let us banish the Powers of Spirit with the Tablet of Union."

Draw the banishing active and passive Spirit pentagrams over the Tablet of Union, using the colors and vibrating the Names as in the opening. Point to the center and say, "In the names and letters of the Tablet of Union, I banish the Powers of Spirit."

Perform the Magick Reverse Circumambulation by circling the Temple widdershins. Imagine a current of white light passing through you, counteracting the deosil current set up in the opening. After three complete turns, return to the west side of the Altar in a widdershins curve. The cylinder of subtle white force should be gone.

Raise the Wand on high and say, "I hereby give license to depart to any and all spirits that may have been attracted by this rite. Return unto your habitations and abodes, harming none on your way. Let there ever be peace between all of you and I and be ready to come again when called. For now, depart!" Knock forcefully with the wand on the altar.

Declare the Temple closed and ring a battery of 3-5-3 with the Bell.

Evocation of the Four Seniors of a Particular Planet or the Four Kings Together – Short Form Ceremony

The short form version of the evocation of four Seniors and Kings together is intended for those magicians who have a great deal of experience with evocation of one angel in full temple. There is no setup or preparation. There are no protections or lead-up to the impact of the power of the Enochian angels when they're summoned. Any beginner in magick who undertakes this method of evocation must take full responsibility for the outcome of her or his efforts.

1. Perform the LBRP.
2. Face north and intone the fifth Enochian call of Earth.
3. Call the Earth Senior of the target planet.
4. Face east and repeat.
5. Repeat for west and south.
6. Be seated and perform systematic body relaxation and rhythmic breathing.
7. Receive the communion of the angels you've called.
8. Face east and give a general license to depart to the spirits.
9. End with the LBRP if desired.

Evocation of the Several Types
of Subangle Angels
Full Temple Ceremony

O	C	A	N	C
A	R	B	I	Z
O	P	A	N	A
D	O	L	O	P
R	X	P	A	O
A	X	T	I	R

The Earth of Earth Subangle
Lower Left Subquadrant of the Earth Tablet

Each of the four Watchtower tablets are divided into four sections, called subangles or subquadrants. Each subangle is attributed to one of the four elements and so a subelement of the tablet's main element. For example, the above subquadrant is the lower left quarter of the Earth tablet and is attributed to Earth. Therefore, the subangle is referred to the Earth of Earth subelement. The subangles of each tablet are attributed to Fire, Water, Air, and

Earth, starting with the lower right quarter, then upper right, then upper left, then lower left, working counterclockwise.

The quarters are separated by the Great Cross of each tablet and are colored differently to set them apart. The squares are colored based on the elemental attribution of the tablet as a whole while the letters are colored based on the subelement of the subangle. For example, the Air of Fire subquadrant of the southern Watchtower has red colored squares and yellow colored letters. Native subangles such as Fire of Fire or Air of Air have letters colored in the complimentary of the element. For example, the Earth of Earth subangle given above has letters colored white, the complimentary of the black of Earth.

The exception to this rule is the cross of six vertical squares and five horizontal squares, which are colored like those of the Great Cross of the tablet. It is called the Calvary Cross. The magical names spelled out by the two bars of this cross refer to angels who are of a higher rank than the subelemental angels of their subquadrant. They are of a more exalted nature, having squares which are colored like those of the Great Cross. For example, the Calvary Cross angels of the Earth of Earth subangle given above are ABALPT and ARBIZ. The six lettered vertical name refers to the summoning angel of the subangle while the five lettered horizontal name refers to the commanding angel.

These angels rule over those whose names are spelled out by the elementally colored squares below the horizontal bar. The four names, broken in half by the vertical bar of the Calvary Cross, refer to the servient angels. The two Calvary Cross angels must be evoked before the servients under their command. These angels in the Earth of Earth subangle given above are OPNA, DOOP, RXAO, and AXIR.

The four elementally colored squares above the horizontal bar, broken up by the vertical bar, form the names of four Kerubic angels. These names are derived by revolving the letters, one at a time. The first Kerubic name is spelled out by the four letters as they appear in the subangle. The second name is derived by moving the first letter to the end of the first name. The third and fourth Kerubic names are derived by continuing this process. For example, the first Kerubic angel name of the Earth of Earth subangle given above is OCNC. The other names are CNCO, NCOC, and COCN.

These angels are ruled by a Kerubic King, whose name is derived by taking the four Kerubic letters as they appear in the subangle and prefixing another letter to them. The traditional method of choosing this letter involves superimposing the version of the Watchtower tablets given to Dee and Kelley in 1587 onto an earlier version, given in 1584. The subelemental attributions to the subangles of the two versions are different and the methods of deriving which letters from the older Watchtowers are used in the newer Watchtower scheme is confusing. The author of this book prefers to simply use the first letter of the Spirit name of the Tablet of Union which relates to the element of the tablet. The Spirit names are EXARP for Air, HCOMA for Water, NANTA for Earth, and BITOM for Fire. For example, the name of the Kerubic King of the Earth of Earth subangle given above is NOCNC. The letter N from NANTA is to be used for all four Kerubic King names of the Earth tablet.

Each subangle of the four Watchtower tablets has its own Enochian call associated with it, except for the four native subquadrants. However, the call associated with the tablet must be intoned first. Then the call of the particular subangle is used to prepare for evoking its angels. Use only the call for the tablet to evoke the angels of the native subangle. For example, only the fifth Enochian call of Earth is to be intoned to prepare for calling any of the angels of the Earth of Earth subquadrant given above. Intone the sixth call of Fire and then the 16th call of Air of Fire to evoke the angels of the Air subangle, upper left, of the Fire tablet.

Evocation:

Set up and open the temple according to the instructions given in the Seniors and Kings evocation ceremony. There is no need for the hexagram ritual in this type of elemental operation. Declare the purpose of the rite, mentioning which angels of which subangle of which tablet are to be summoned.

Walk to the East with wand in hand and then proceed around the temple to the tablet whose angels are to be evoked. Point with the wand to the center of the Watchtower and intone the associated Enochian call. If the target subangle is not native to the tablet, point with the wand to the center of the subquadrant and intone its associated call.

Evoke the two Calvary Cross angels or the Kerubic King as appropriate and then the servient or Kerubic angels, as the case may be. Trace each name with the wand while intoning the same. One, several, or all of the servient or Kerubic angels may be evoked together. The author of this book has found great value in calling all four of each type to achieve a full vision of the intelligences associated with the related subelement.

Declare, "I shall now commune with the angels thus evoked." Sit in a comfortable position, relax the body from head to toe, perform some rhythmic breathing, and then open the mind's eye to receive the vision and power of the conjured angels. When you're satisfied with the results of the contact, exit the vision and return to body consciousness. Go to the west side of the altar and face East.

Take up the wand and banish the angels by declaring, "I hereby give <angel names> license to depart. Return unto your habitations and abodes. Let there ever be peace between you and I and be ready to come again when called. For now, depart!" Give one sharp rap on the altar with the wand. Proceed to the closing.

Further Operations with the lesser angels of the subangles:

There are sixteen subangles on the four Watchtower tablets and so a total of thirty-two Calvary Cross angels, sixty-four servient angels, sixteen Kerubic Kings, and sixty-four Kerubic angels. Evoking all the lesser angels of a particular tablet will reveal a great deal about the nature of the associated element in all its divisions and manifestations. Working with the servients and/or the Kerubics of the four native subangles gives an excellent introduction to the nature of the Enochian lesser angels with a minimum of memorization required.

John Dee specified a complex method of working with the subangle angels in his magical diary as published in *The Enochian Magic of Dr. John Dee* by Geoffrey James. Eight different workings are described wherein a particular subangle of all four tablets and either the servient or Kerubic angels of those subquadrants are chosen to develop a particular magical power. For example, the servient angels of the Earth subangles of each of the Watchtowers are called together in one operation to gain the power of transformation. This evocation involves eight Calvary Cross angels and sixteen servient angels, all considered to be angels of transformation. The recommended order of evocation is Earth of Earth, Earth of Air, Earth of Water, and Earth of Fire. The angels themselves will have to instruct the magician as to how their transformative power is to be wielded and to what it can be applied.

The eight lesser angelic types are as follows:

Earth of subangles – Kerubics: Mechanical Arts
Earth of subangles – servients: Transformation
Air of subangles – Kerubics: Natural Substances
Air of subangles – servients: Medicine
Water of subangles – Kerubics: Transportation
Water of subangles – servients: Metals and Jewels
Fire of subangles – Kerubics: Secret Discovery
Fire of subangles – servients: Knowledge of the Elements

The author of this book cannot guarantee success in developing any of the powers specified by Dee. Frequent evocation may bring some success, according to the abilities of the individual magician. At least, a great deal of knowledge and ceremonial acumen will be gained.

All Elementals Evocation Ceremony

This ceremony is intended to evoke the five elemental hierarchies, from the lowliest spirit to the most exalted angelic ruler. It is done without temple setup or preparation. The magician is free to work with any type of elemental spirit that answers this freeform, holistic evocation. Memorization of the first six Enochian calls is optional but recommended. The novice in magick is urged not to perform this ceremony until a good deal of training is had.

1. Perform the LBRP and intone the first Enochian call.
2. Face north and say, "I hereby open the gate of the north and evoke all angels, elementals, and spirits of Earth. Come forth to this place and time and join with your fellow spirits in communion. Join me and together, we will achieve a greater destiny. Harken unto my call."
3. Intone the fifth Enochian call of Earth.
4. Call the Great King of the north and Earth, ICZHIHAL. Feel his presence to the fullest extent and unite the entire Earth spiritual hierarchy in one flowing energy.
5. Turn to face east and open the gate of the east and Air. Intone the third Enochian call of Air and call the Air King, BATAIVAH. Fuse the flood of Air energy with the Earth

      energy from the north. Achieve union of Earth and Air in full communion.

6. Turn to the west and repeat the process for Water and RAAGIOSL.
7. Turn to the south and repeat the process for Fire and EDLPRNAA.
8. Turn to the east and intone the second Enochian call of Spirit.
9. Call the Spirit of Spirit angel, EHNB.
10. Achieve complete union of all five elemental fusions. Either meditate or perform a dance to move with the complex flow of astral energy.

The elemental fusion may be fixed in a talisman or statue for the purposes of creating an oracle. Frequent repetition may result in Abramelin like results. The magician may use the evocations and results according to Will.

Evocation of the Thirty Aethyrs

The four elemental Watchtower tablets are conceived to be sides of a cosmic cube in the Enochian model of reality. Its top and bottom consist of the Sigillum dei Aemeth and another design derived from John Dee's magick. This cube is surrounded by thirty concentric spheres, conceived of as planes of existence beyond the physical. They are numbered from thirty to one, going from the innermost to the outermost sphere. The thirtieth air or plane is closest in nature to the physical world while the first aethyr has the most transcendent of natures.

Each aethyr has a name of three Enochian letters and contains three governing angels, except for the thirtieth, which contains four. There are thus a total of ninety-one governors whose names are derived in complex ways from letters of the four Watchtower tablets. A sigil for each governor is created by connecting these letters with lines. Consult *Enochian Vision Magick* by Lon DuQuette to see what these sigils look like.

An aethyr may be evoked by intoning the nineteenth Enochian call. The name of the aethyr to be called is inserted into the first line. The nineteenth call is thereby conceived of as being thirty different calls, making a total of forty-eight calls, along with the six elemental and twelve subelemental calls. Dee wrote that there is a silent call that comes before any of the others, so there are actually forty-nine calls in all. The number seven is featured prominently throughout the various magical systems developed by John Dee and Edward Kelley and so it is with the aethyrs. Note that 91 = 7 * 13 and 30 aethyrs plus five elemental tablets gives 35 = 7 * 5.

The magician may use the formal temple setup and opening to prepare for aethyr evocation or simply perform a LBRP, intoning the nineteenth call, and receiving the vision thereof. In *The Vision and the Voice*, Crowley stared into a shewstone and skryed each aethyr. In fact, this shewstone was exactly the one used by John Dee and Edward Kelley over three centuries earlier. The method promoted in this book is to enter into a meditative state and use the mind's eye to skry into the magick mirror of the imagination.

The names of the Thirty Aethyrs and their governors are as follows:

LIL	First Aethyr
ARN	Second Aethyr
ZOM	Third Aethyr
PAZ	Fourth Aethyr
LIT	Fifth Aethyr
MAZ	Sixth Aethyr
DEO	Seventh Aethyr
ZID	Eighth Aethyr
ZIP	Ninth Aethyr
ZAX	Tenth Aethyr
ICH	Eleventh Aethyr

LOE	Twelfth Aethyr
ZIM	Thirteenth Aethyr
UTA	Fourteenth Aethyr
OXO	Fifteenth Aethyr
LEA	Sixteenth Aethyr
TAN	Seventeenth Aethyr
ZEN	Eighteenth Aethyr
POP	Nineteenth Aethyr
KHR	Twentieth Aethyr
ASP	Twenty First Aethyr
LIN	Twenty Second Aethyr
TOR	Twenty Third Aethyr
NIA	Twenty Fourth Aethyr
UTI	Twenty Fifth Aethyr
DES	Twenty Sixth Aethyr
ZAA	Twenty Seventh Aethyr
BAG	Twenty Eighth Aethyr
RII	Twenty Ninth Aethyr
TEX	Thirtieth Aethyr
OCCODON	Governor of the First Aethyr
PASCOMB	Governor of the First Aethyr
VALGARS	Governor of the First Aethyr
DOAGNIS	Governor of the Second Aethyr
PACASNA	Governor of the Second Aethyr
DIALIVA	Governor of the Second Aethyr
SAMAPHA	Governor of the Third Aethyr
VIROOLI	Governor of the Third Aethyr
ANDISPI	Governor of the Third Aethyr
THOTANF	Governor of the Fourth Aethyr

AXZIARG   Governor of the Fourth Aethyr
POTHNIR   Governor of the Fourth Aethyr

LAZDIXI   Governor of the Fifth Aethyr
NOCAMAL   Governor of the Fifth Aethyr
TIARPAX   Governor of the Fifth Aethyr

SAXTOMP   Governor of the Sixth Aethyr
VAVAAMP   Governor of the Sixth Aethyr
ZIRZIRD   Governor of the Sixth Aethyr
OBMACAS   Governor of the Seventh Aethyr

GENADOL   Governor of the Seventh Aethyr
ASPIAON   Governor of the Seventh Aethyr

ZAMFRES   Governor of the Eighth Aethyr
TODNAON   Governor of the Eighth Aethyr
PRISTAC   Governor of the Eighth Aethyr

ODDIORG   Governor of the Ninth Aethyr
CRALPIR   Governor of the Ninth Aethyr
DOANZIN   Governor of the Ninth Aethyr

LEXARPH   Governor of the Tenth Aethyr
COMANAN   Governor of the Tenth Aethyr
TABITOM   Governor of the Tenth Aethyr

MOLPAND   Governor of the Eleventh Aethyr
VANARDA   Governor of the Eleventh Aethyr
PONODOL   Governor of the Eleventh Aethyr

TAPAMAL   Governor of the Twelfth Aethyr
GEDOONS   Governor of the Twelfth Aethyr

AMBRIAL   Governor of the Twelfth Aethyr

GECAOND   Governor of the Thirteenth Aethyr
LAPARIN   Governor of the Thirteenth Aethyr
DOCEPAX   Governor of the Thirteenth Aethyr

TEDOOND   Governor of the Fourteenth Aethyr
VIVIPOS   Governor of the Fourteenth Aethyr
OOANAMB   Governor of the Fourteenth Aethyr

TAHANDO   Governor of the Fifteenth Aethyr
NOCIABI   Governor of the Fifteenth Aethyr
TASTOXO   Governor of the Fifteenth Aethyr

COCARPT   Governor of the Sixteenth Aethyr
LANACON   Governor of the Sixteenth Aethyr
SOCHIAL   Governor of the Sixteenth Aethyr

SIGMORF   Governor of the Seventeenth Aethyr
AYDROPT   Governor of the Seventeenth Aethyr
TOCARZI   Governor of the Seventeenth Aethyr

NABAOMI   Governor of the Eighteenth Aethyr
ZAFASAI   Governor of the Eighteenth Aethyr
YALPAMB   Governor of the Eighteenth Aethyr

TORZOXI   Governor of the Nineteenth Aethyr
ΛBAIOND   Governor of the Nineteenth Aethyr
OMAGRAP   Governor of the Nineteenth Aethyr

ZILDRON   Governor of the Twentieth Aethyr
PARZIBA   Governor of the Twentieth Aethyr
TOTOCAN   Governor of the Twentieth Aethyr

CHIRSPA	Governor of the Twenty First Aethyr
TOANTOM	Governor of the Twenty First Aethyr
VIXPALG	Governor of the Twenty First Aethyr
OZIDAIA	Governor of the Twenty Second Aethyr
PARAOAN	Governor of the Twenty Second Aethyr
CALZIRG	Governor of the Twenty Second Aethyr
RONOAMB	Governor of the Twenty Third Aethyr
ONIZIMP	Governor of the Twenty Third Aethyr
ZAXANIN	Governor of the Twenty Third Aethyr
ORCAMIR	Governor of the Twenty Fourth Aethyr
CHIALPS	Governor of the Twenty Fourth Aethyr
SOAGEEL	Governor of the Twenty Fourth Aethyr
MIRZIND	Governor of the Twenty Fifth Aethyr
OBUAORS	Governor of the Twenty Fifth Aethyr
RANGLAM	Governor of the Twenty Fifth Aethyr
POPHAND	Governor of the Twenty Sixth Aethyr
NIGRANA	Governor of the Twenty Sixth Aethyr

BAZCHIM   Governor of the Twenty Sixth Aethyr

SAZIAMI   Governor of the Twenty Seventh Aethyr

MATHVLA   Governor of the Twenty Seventh Aethyr

ORPAMB   Governor of the Twenty Seventh Aethyr

LABNIXP   Governor of the Twenty Eighth Aethyr

FOCISNI   Governor of the Twenty Eighth Aethyr

OXLOPAR   Governor of the Twenty Eighth Aethyr

VASTRIM   Governor of the Twenty Ninth Aethyr

ODRAXTI   Governor of the Twenty Ninth Aethyr

GOMZIAM   Governor of the Twenty Ninth Aethyr

TAONGLA   Governor of the Thirtieth Aethyr
GEMNIMB   Governor of the Thirtieth Aethyr
ADVORPT   Governor of the Thirtieth Aethyr
DOZINAL   Governor of the Thirtieth Aethyr

CHAPTER 10
RESULTS

ADVANCED ENOCHIAN EVOCATIONS

Evocation of the four Mercury Seniors of Earth, Air, Water, and Fire: AHMLICV, AVTOTAR, SONIZNT, and ANODOIN

The Earth Senior appeared in vision as a classic angelic figure in a gray robe, almost a black and white figure. The Air Senior appeared in hypercolored glory in a flashing robe, surrounded by clouds. The Water Senior appeared as a whirl of thick, black color, too big to fit in the western quarter of the temple. He was partially in the room and partially outside of it. The Fire Senior appeared as a column and whirl of flame, ever in coruscating motion. Only a small aspect of his mighty being could fit in the southern quarter of the temple. These manifestations of elemental superconsciousness communicated the following insights to me.

AHMLICV told me that the function of Mercury in Earth was to bring cosmic intent, the Will of the living, intelligent universe, into manifestation. This action is seen in the shapes taken by matter throughout the universe on all scales. The patterns of galaxies can be seen in sea shells, various plants, hurricanes, etc. Nature takes on forms in specific patterns that have been called archetypes, a correlate idea to that of the psychologist, Carl Jung's theory of racial collective archetypes. The human psyche is based on root patterns of experience which are recognized in dreams and visions, just as natural systems take on certain basic forms. The spirals, waves, and dendrites of large scale matter reveal the consciousness inherent in all of reality, just as archetypal symbols like wheels, the sun, and family figures reveal the core of human consciousness.

All of this manifests by the Will of the totality of all things, the cosmos as one coherent entity. This is the holographic model of reality. The connections underlying all manifestation constitute the intelligence that concretizes as minds and systems of matter on all scales of size. The whole exists throughout each and every part of itself. The cosmos grows more intelligent as human minds and material systems gain greater complexity, forming new shapes and ideas. The feedback between whole and part is continuous, driving evolution and intelligence increase.

AVTOTAR said that the power of Mercury in Air brings the impress of cosmic intent into the human psyche and other systems of subatomic activity. The universal mind comes to the individual as a storm out of the east to take shape as a messenger of the eternal spirit. The intrinsic archetypes of nature and the collective archetypes of humanity are built at this level and transmitted throughout all of reality by the omnipresence of the holographic totality.

SONIZNT revealed a shadow of that aspect of the universe which is purely unknowable. The power of Mercury in Water is to concentrate coherent possibility out of the immutable, undifferentiated nature of the cosmos. The potential for actualization in organized forms based on cosmic archetypal memory is drawn out of pure chaos by the Mercurial Will to create. The lightning of creative Will emerges out of the unfathomable darkness of pure nothingness as a spontaneous act of the whole of reality. The Light of Intelligence arises out of pure nullity.

ANODOIN indicated by its whirling motions and emanations that the power of Mercury in Fire was a synergy of all archetypal unfoldments of intelligence in the universe. The sum total of all emergence of order at all scales comes together in a transcendent state of becoming that encompasses and interpenetrates the whole of reality. True genius draws from this metalevel of intelligence. The shining star and the human genius of science and art both express the brilliance of the ultimate transcendence.

I brought all four angels together into one comprehensive communication and communion to discover the true nature of Mercury among the elements. They came together to form a great bolt of lightning that shot up from the floor. Then, I understood that the influence of Mercury among the elements and in the universe acted as a bolt of lightning shining in the darkness. This was the first impulse of creation from the pure nothingness of chaos. The first intrinsic archetype was established, allowing for all the basic patterns of material and psychic unfoldment to emerge. The core cosmic intelligence lends itself to all ordered nature, evolving to ever greater complexity by the feedback across all planes and scales of being. Human genius is the inevitable evolution of the cosmic creative process. The transcendent consciousness of the new age has come from the full recognition of feedback with the totality of existence.

Evocation of the angels of the Earth of Earth subangle and the Fire of Fire subangle:

ABALPT and ARBIZ, the Calvary Cross angels of the Earth of Earth subangle, appeared in vision as a white cross of flame in the midst of a pitch black space. They spoke in unison to say that they could call the Earth of Earth servient angels, reveal past events related to Earth, and shine as a beacon of light in the darkness.

The servient angels, OPNA, DOOP, RXAO, and AXIR, appeared as four identical gnomes with human faces. They told me in unison that they could call the Earth elemental energies and shape them to my Will. I told them to do so and they generated a huge, multidimensional wave which seemed to cause my temple floor to become wavy, like a choppy ocean. The servients then caused these waves to focus into a tall tower of shimmering force coming up out of the floor. Nothing physical was actually disturbed but the underlying nature of the space of my temple seemed to become malleable.

The Kerubic angels, OCNC, CNCO, NCOC, and COCN, were summoned next, by the Will of their King. They appeared together as a circular motion of white light against a black background. With four voices at once, they told me that their nature was to give form to all matter by entering into it and holding it together as a coherent whole. Each object is a whole until itself, existing in the greater wholeness of the universe. Reality consists of holograms within holograms in a complex hierarchy of continuous feedback of pattern transference.

They act in concert with the Kerubic angels of the Earth subangles of the other tablets to manifest pure idea, to bring together matter according to the intrinsic archetypes. Real power in matter is developed thereby.

I here note that the two groups of four angels act together as parts of a greater whole. Their individual value is limited. No wonder Dee asserted that four groups of these angelic types from the four Watchtower tablets produce greater power in concert.

RZIONR and NRZFM, the Calvary Cross angels of the Fire of Fire subangle, appeared at first as darting yellow and red flames coming out of the Fire tablet. Soon, they coalesced into a flaming cross in front of me as seen by my mind's eye. Their wordless communication was that they work their will, derived directly from the Tablet of Union, to conjure and control the servient angels of their subangle. They, like all Calvary Cross angels, express the Will of the Tablet of Union in their element and their tablet generally, being the purest expression of their element. Their power can charge talismans dedicated to Fire which have their names written in a cross pattern like in their subangle. All Calvary Cross angels can do this for their respective elements.

The servient angels, ADRE, SISP, PALI, and ACAR, appeared immediately before me as four concentric circles of flame. They continually exchanged essence with each other so that their identities shifted constantly. Their mutual circulation communicated to me that their nature was to move all things that move. Nothing can move across space through time without their active intervention. They are movement itself. This means that all motion consists of a holistic readjustment of all the dimensions of reality.

The Kerubic angels, ZIZA, IZAZ, ZAZI, and AZIZ, came out of the Fire tablet as four balls of flame which settled before me in a diamond formation. Lines of flame erupted from the balls to connect them as a diamond. The formation rotated clockwise as the angels spoke, one shift to the right for each word. Sometimes during their speech, the diamond flipped 180 degrees forward. Their nature is to increase the energy and intensity of all things, energizing inertia into greater activity. They are the essence of continuing expansion and increasing intensity. The servients raise the energy of a system to a certain fixed level but the Kerubics yield ever quickening power. This ever increasing movement tends to lead to dynamic stability, allowing for greater order to emerge from chaos.

Evocation of all elemental powers through the use of the first six Enochian calls and the angelic elemental Kings:

The Earth elementals appeared as little motes of dust whirling around chaotically. ICZHIHAL expanded everything, including the containing space, to a broader dimension. A greater totality was realized, a cohesiveness to space and time that revealed a continuous ocean of being.

The Air elementals came through the invisible gate as whirling balls of color. The Air call exploded from me, from every nerve and fiber of my mind and body. The balls became streams of whirling hypercolors in an infinite sky full of fluffy clouds. BATAIVAH appeared as a vast pillar of yellow hypercolor flowing up through my body and out to the sky scene. A state of delighted ecstasy flooded my consciousness, making every nerve stream with yellow joy.

Earth and Air fused to mix dust and streams. The expanded earthly and heavenly dimensions came together to build a plenum of in between spaces reaching from inside my mind to outside my body and out to the broader magical states of being. The sense of life in matter became pronounced as my entire being was raised to a higher pitch of living activity.

The Water elementals were as one cosmic space flooding the Earth and Air dimensions to inundate them in an even greater state of being. It felt like the entire cosmos was present in the temple. The Water call intensified everything to a higher pitch of ecstasy, yielding a sense of inviolable peace. This was different from the angelic Air ecstasy, which drew from great excitation. RAAGIOSL absorbed my entire being, every particle and sensation, in an ecstasy of pure, complete totality that dissolved my sense of self. The cosmic wholeness was the only existence. Earth and Air were dust lost in nothingness.

I came back to myself enough to open the Fire gate in the south. A bolt of solid lightning appeared to my mind's eye in the temple, shooting from lower left to upper right at a slight angle. This was clearly a tiny piece of a flow of energy so far beyond the four dimensions of space and time that it carried my senses to a yet broader state of space than anything else to this point in the evocation. A greater feedback began as multicolored lightning patterns entered my personal space, moving slowly toward me. At a certain point, they stopped and my entire sense of space dissolved in a continuity of existence wherein all dimensions so far realized flowed through each other as one undifferentiated state of being.

The Fire call did little to intensify this state of pure impersonal transcendence. A great deal was happening in my unconscious which couldn't be rendered by the functions of my personal awareness. EDLPRNAA immediately intensified my entire vision state into a seething hyperblue fire conflagration. There was too much going on for me to make sense of it all. I dwelt in a state of pure, transcendent hyperfire for a time and then turned to face east.

Elemental Spirit turned everything into a peaceful, white state. All the other elements were left behind in this greater transcendence, detached from all specific conditions. The second Spirit call yielded a sense of love and unity to all existence. EHNB stepped out of my body and everything turned into white powder. It seemed to cover all the furniture of the temple as well as my body. I felt it inside me. The white powder and space were the totalities which give birth to the possibility of material condition in matter, energy, space, time, and consciousness. It seemed as if any new creation was possible by manipulation of the Spirit reality.

I returned to normal waking consciousness to record my experiences in my magical diary. I felt cleansed, focused, and transformed at a subtle level of being that just barely registered to my awareness. More practice was needed to refine my control over the titanic forces of the Enochian universe that had become available to me through years of steady practice in more formal settings. Mysticism and magick had become parts of a greater spectrum of my evocatory experience. Now, there was just increasing natural growth toward the ultimate transcendence.

Evocations of the 30th Aethyr:

I have not yet evoked any of the thirty aethyrs myself. However, I've attended various seminars on Enochian magick and have witnessed others performing these evocations. So far, I've witnessed three simple ceremonies calling the 30th aethyr, TEX, by the nineteenth Enochian call. Here is a summary of my experiences in these public settings.

The first vision revealed a pure white space. The essence of reality shone through the entire vision in brilliant white gleamings. It felt very much like my second ENHB vision, a revelation of the transcendent Limitless Light. However, nothing happened.

The state was static and beatific. Others in attendance reported having only vague hints of action in various contexts. Clearly, the aethyrs are beyond the reach of most magicians.

The second occasion produced a similar space and state of being but this time there was a central object. It was a shining, golden cup reminiscent of the Holy Graal of Arthurian legends. The meaning of the vision was that the source of all cosmic creation resided in the Limitless Light. The transcendent, unfocusable state of unlimited dimensional expansion attains an impossible, paradoxical focus to allow the process of continuous creation of an ordered, dimensionally specific cosmos to occur.

My third vision of the 30th aethyr revealed the same brilliant white space as before. Something else happened after a few minutes, however. The entire scene spontaneously turned pitch black. I moved through the space for a short while and then I came upon a large red Valentine's heart with three swords thrust through it. This symbol can be seen on the Three of Swords card in traditional tarot decks.

I understood this heart-sword symbol as cognate to the Holy Graal of my previous vision of the 30th aethyr. An aspect of the ever shifting, chaotic dimensional expansion of the Limitless Light brilliance is the null darkness of pure chaos. Opposites are aspects of each other in the transcendent states of reality. This observation supports Crowley's assertion that contradiction is unity above the Abyss on the Tree of Life. It is in this alternate, opposite state that a specific process of cosmic creation may emerge from pure nothingness. The focus of emergence is the fount of all being, source of all that was, is, and shall be.

Other cognate symbols to the Graal and the heart stabbed with three swords are the Solar-Phallus and the Chi-Rho. This last symbol consists of what looks like the English letter P superimposed on a capital X. These are the Greek letters, chi and rho. It has been called the monogram of Christ by Christian Qabalists but there are inherent ideas with this symbol which predate Christianity. These letters look like an equal armed cross with a line rising from the center when looked at from an angle. The line is topped with a hook, like an inversion of direction back toward the cross. The rho, like the Hebrew resh, is attributed to the sun and suggests a dimension that is transcendent to the normally perceived world as represented by the cross of the elements. The alchemical meaning is a realization of consciousness on a higher than physical level. In my vision, the meaning was clear that the force of initiation toward the source of creation is the same as the force that brings that creation into being. In the ancient Egyptian religion, these superimposed symbols can be seen as the crook and scourge held by the Pharaoh. He is the symbol of the God-man, the ideal of spiritual transcendence realized in later ages as Christ and Krishna. The Chi-Rho can be studied in greater detail in Eliphas Levi's book, *The Magical Ritual of the Sanctum Regnum.*

CHAPTER 11
CULMINATION

THE THELEMIC ADEPT SELF INITIATION CEREMONY

Preparation:

Set up a double cubed Altar in the middle of a square or rectangular room. Place a pedestal in the center of each wall, marking out the four quarters of existence. Each direction is infinite and reaches into a higher than physical world. The reaches of infinity focus on the central altar from the east, south, west, north, above, and below. Thus, the altar is the center of the universe, the point of balance from which any energy may be launched to cause any effect anywhere.

Let the Altar, symbolizing the consciousness of the magician, center of his/her universe, be covered with a black cloth draping down on all sides to touch the floor or let it be painted black. Place the four elemental weapons on top of the Altar, answering to the elemental natures of the quarters, symbolized by the four elements of classical Greek science: Air, Fire, Water, and Earth. Thus, place the Air Dagger on the eastern side of the altar, place the Fire Wand on the southern side, place the Water Cup filled with water on the western side, and place the Earth Pentacle on the northern side. In the center, the center of All, place a flask of fragrant Oil, symbolizing the ubiquitous element of Spirit. Oil of cinnamon or Abramelin oil are appropriate. A favored Holy Book may be placed underneath the flask if desired. In this way, the magician is expressed as a microcosm, an entire universe in miniature, whose several natures correspond to the forces of creation.

Place a Censor on the southern side of the Altar or the southern pedestal as desired, burning frankincense and myrrh, incense of Abramelin, or other relevant incense. Place the Bell at any convenient spot. Embellish the Altar with crystals, black, white, or multicolored tapers, etc.

Each pedestal marks the nature of its quarter, indicating the frequency of magical power emanating from that particular infinity. Mark the nature of Air in the east by placing an emblem of that which rules the airy nature such as the Angelic Air Tablet. Place a white votive candle in front of the tablet to light the darkling, mysterious abyss of the east. Place an emblem of the element itself with the candle, such as a hand fan or rose. Place the Angelic Spirit Tablet, called the Tablet of Union, in the far east raised above the other tablets.

In the south, place the symbols of Fire: the Angelic Fire Tablet, a white votive, and a red lamp, red candle, or candle in a red holder. In the west, place the symbols of Water: the Angelic Water Tablet, a white votive, and a cup or bowl of pure water. In the north, place the symbols of Earth: the Angelic Earth Tablet, a white votive, and a plate of salt.

Also, place the higher octave elemental weapons: the Sword, the Staff, the Chalice, and the Lamp, at appropriate stations around the magick temple. The Lamp of Spirit can hang above the altar, the higher octave emblem of Earth, or in the far east. Place the Staff of Fire in the south, the Chalice of Water in the west, and the Sword of Air in the east or other convenient spot.

Place the seven planetary Major Arcana Tarot cards around the magick temple at the points of an imaginary planetary heptagram whose single downward point is in the west. Place the Saturn card, The Universe, in the west and then place the other cards in Qabalistic order around the temple.[1] Place emblems of the three alchemical elements at the corners of an imaginary triangle whose points are in the east (Mercury), southwest (Sulfur), and northwest (Salt). Use a red candle for Sulfur, a paten of salt or bread for Salt, and a book of scripture, white candle, or lantern for Mercury. In this way, the cross of the elements is placed within the triangle of spiritual

---

[1] Consult *The Book of Thoth*, by The Master Therion, page 11, for a diagram of the planetary heptagram.

aspiration, all of which is contained within the celestial realm of the planets and stars. Everything remains centered and focused on the altar as the seed-source.

In the east, place Atu XIV, a Lamen of Luna, a Lamen of Sol, and the Keystone of the Mysteries of Initiation, each hidden in a box. Place a Pentagram Lamen on the altar. It is up to the magician to purchase or fashion these objects based on the totality of her/his magical experiences and understanding.

Prepare the water in the Cup on the altar by dropping a few particles of salt into it and say, "May the salt of Earth admonish the Waters to bear the virtue of the Great Sea." Let the candles of the magick temple be lit.

Astral Temple Visualization and Auric Preparation:

Take three deep breaths to calm your mood and focus your attention. Close your eyes and visualize your body of light detach from your physical body and begin to rise upward. Reach the ceiling of your physical temple and then move through it. Continue rising above your home, high into the air with ever increasing speed. See the clouds fly by you as your energy body reaches beyond the earth's atmosphere.

Launch yourself with a great burst of acceleration into outer space, leaving the entire planet earth far behind. The sun becomes just a point of light in the midst of the darkness of the void, one among myriad others. Travel lightyears in seconds with the speed of thought as you finally reach the cosmic temple, set amidst the vastness of deep space. It is in the shape of a torus, like a huge donut. Each wheel of that greater wheel is a flow of brilliant white light. A current of blue power flows through the middle of all these wheels on the same plane as the torus as a whole. All the furniture and implements of the physical temple are placed in the central space surrounded by the wheel of wheels with the altar in the center of all. A spike of downward shooting brilliant white light passes through the middle of the altar, an axle of the wheel.

Move your body of light to the west side of the astral altar facing the east of the temple and perform a Middle Pillar Exercise or a Rousing of the Citadels ritual. Visualize a ball of brilliant white light above your head, its bottom point touching the top of your head. Vibrate the divine Name AHIH three times, pronounced as Ehayay.

Send a shaft of brilliant white light downward from the crown sphere, through your head, to your neck. Visualize a grayish white ball of light there and vibrate the divine Name IHVH ALHIM three times, pronounced as Yahweh Elohim.

Continue the shaft of light downward to the center of your chest and visualize a golden yellow ball there. Vibrate the divine Name IHVH ALVH VDOT three times, pronounced as Yahweh Eloah Va Dot.

Continue the shaft of light downward to a point two inches below your navel and visualize a violet ball of light there. Vibrate the divine Name ShDI AL ChAI three times, pronounced as Shaddaiee El Chaiee.

Continue the shaft of light downward to a point between your feet. Visualize an olive green ball there, half above the floor of the temple and half below. Vibrate the divine Name ADNI HARTz three times, pronounced as Adonaiee Ha Aretz.

Reinforce the visualization of all five colored balls with the connecting shaft of light and feel the integration of all the energy in your physical and light bodies. Start a current of energy moving from the top of your head down the front of your body to your feet and then back to the top of your head from behind. Send energy down the right side of your body and then up the left. Raise a stream of energy from your feet up the central shaft of visualization to your head and then out the top in a shower of sparks that fall all around your body. Finally, feel all the energies and currents of your physical and light bodies reach out to the farthest stars to establish a universal connection. You are now ready to do magick as a complete microcosm, a true mirror of all that was, is, and shall be.

Opening:

Stand on the west side of the Altar, facing east. Perform the Lesser Banishing Ritual of the Pentagram or the Star Ruby.

Purify the Temple by taking the Cup, moving to the east wall, raising the Cup on high, and saying, "For pure will, unassuaged of purpose, delivered from the lust of result, is every way perfect."[2]

Bring the Cup to heart level and say, "By the Lustral Water of the Loud Resounding Sea, I purify this Temple and all persons and objects within." Mark the points of an inverted triangle with the Cup, upper left, upper right, then lower center. Imagine an inverted blue triangle hanging in midair.

Walk deosil to the south quarter and repeat the above paragraph. Repeat for west and north, return to the east, and walk back to the west side of the Altar in a deosil curve.

Consecrate the Temple by taking up the fuming Censor, moving to the east wall, raising the Censor on high, and saying, "So that thy light is in me; & its red flame is as a sword in my hand to push thy order."[3]

---

[2] Liber Legis, Chapter 1, Verse 44
[3] Liber Legis, Chapter 3, Verse 38

Bring the Censor to heart level and say, "With the Sacred Fire which darts and flashes through the hidden depths of the universe, I consecrate this Temple and all persons and objects within." Mark the points of an upright triangle by swinging the Censor toward the upper center, lower left, then lower right. Ideally, a puff of smoke should be left when the Censor swings away from the point. Imagine a red triangle superimposed on the blue triangle, making a hexagram.

Walk deosil to the south quarter and repeat the above paragraph. Repeat for west and north, return to the east, and walk back to the west side of the altar in a deosil curve. Replace the Censor and take up the Wand.

Open each of the Angelic Tablets in turn, from east through south, west, and north as follows. Stand before the eastern tablet with Wand in hand. Say, "Let us evoke the Powers of Air with the Great Eastern Quadrangle."

Draw the invoking active spirit pentagram in black against a white background over the tablet, point to the center, and vibrate AHIH and then EXARP. Draw the invoking Air pentagram in violet against a yellow background, vibrating IHVH. Put down the Wand, take up the Fan, and draw the Kerubic sign of Aquarius in violet within the Air pentagram, creating a wind with the Fan. Vibrate Raphael and visualize Him standing behind the tablet.

Replace the Fan, take up the Wand, and draw a golden cross over the Great Cross of the tablet from top to bottom and then left to right. Draw a deosil golden circle around the cross starting from the top point. Point to the center of the cross and say, "In the names and letters of the Great Eastern Quadrangle, I call forth the Powers of Air."

Hold the Wand on high and say, "In the Three Great Secret Names that are borne upon the Banners of the East, (trace the letters of the horizontal line of the Great Cross with the Wand as each Name is vibrated) ORO IBAH AOZPI, I call forth the Powers of Air."

Hold the Wand on high and say, "In the Name of (trace the letters spiraling out from the center) BATAIVAH, great King of the East, I call forth the Powers of Air." Knock.

Go to the southern tablet with Wand in hand. Say, "Let us evoke the Powers of Fire with the Great Southern Quadrangle."

Draw the invoking active spirit pentagram in black against a white background over the tablet, point to the center, and vibrate AHIH and then BITOM. Draw the invoking Fire pentagram in green against a red background, vibrating ALHIM. Put down the Wand, take up the Red Lamp, and draw the Kerubic sign of Leo in green within the Fire pentagram. Vibrate Michael and visualize Him standing behind the tablet.

Replace the Lamp, take up the Wand, and draw a golden cross over the Great Cross of the tablet from top to bottom and then left to right. Draw a deosil golden circle around the cross. Point to the center of the cross and say, "In the names and letters of the Great Southern Quadrangle, I call forth the Powers of Fire."

Hold the Wand on high and say, "In the Three Great Secret Names that are borne upon the Banners of the South, (trace the letters of the horizontal line of the Great Cross with the wand as each Name is vibrated) OIP TEAA PDOCE, I call forth the Powers of Fire."

Hold the Wand on high and say, "In the Name of (trace the letters spiraling out from the center) EDLPRNAA, great King of the South, I call forth the Powers of Fire." Knock.

Go to the western tablet with Wand in hand. Say, "Let us evoke the Powers of Water with the Great Western Quadrangle."

Draw the invoking passive spirit pentagram in white against a black background over the tablet, point to the center, and vibrate Atah Geboor Leolahm Adonai and then HCOMA. Draw the invoking Water pentagram in orange against a blue background, vibrating AL. Put down the Wand, take up the Cup, and draw the Kerubic sign of Scorpio in orange within the Water pentagram. Vibrate Gabriel and visualize Him standing behind the tablet.

Replace the Cup, take up the Wand, and draw a golden cross over the Great Cross of the tablet from top to bottom and then left to right. Draw a deosil golden circle around the cross. Point to the center of the cross and say, "In the names and letters of the Great Western Quadrangle, I call forth the Powers of Water."

Hold the Wand on high and say, "In the Three Great Secret Names that are borne upon the Banners of the West, (trace the letters of the horizontal line of the Great Cross with the Wand as each Name is vibrated) MPH ARSL GAIOL, I call forth the Powers of Water."

Hold the Wand on high and say, "In the Name of (trace the letters spiraling out from the center) RAAGIOSL, great King of the West, I call forth the Powers of Water." Knock.

Go to the northern tablet with Wand in hand. Say, "Let us evoke the Powers of Earth with the Great Northern Quadrangle."

Draw the invoking passive spirit pentagram in white against a black background over the tablet, point to the center, and vibrate Atah Geboor Leolahm Adonai and then NANTA. Draw the invoking Earth pentagram in white against a black background, vibrating ADNI. Put down the Wand, take up the Pentacle, and draw the Kerubic sign of Taurus in white within the Earth pentagram. Vibrate Auriel and visualize Him standing behind the tablet.

Replace the Pentacle, take up the Wand, and draw a golden cross over the Great Cross of the tablet from top to bottom and then left to right. Draw a deosil golden circle around the cross. Point to the center of the cross and say, "In the names and letters of the Great Northern Quadrangle, I call forth the Powers of Earth."

Hold the Wand on high and say, "In the Three Great Secret Names that are borne upon the Banners of the North, (trace the letters of the horizontal line of the Great Cross with the wand as each Name is vibrated) MOR DIAL HCTGA, I call forth the Powers of Earth."

Hold the Wand on high and say, "In the Name of (trace the letters spiraling out from the center) ICZHIHAL, great King of the North, I call forth the Powers of Earth." Knock.

Complete the circle and return to the west side of the Altar, facing east. Say, "Let us evoke the Powers of Spirit with the Tablet of Union."

Draw the invoking passive spirit pentagram in white against a black background over the Tablet of Union, point to the center, and vibrate Atah Geboor Leolahm Adonai. Draw the invoking active spirit pentagram in black against a white background and vibrate AHIH. Vibrate EXARP HCOMA NANTA BITOM, tracing the letters with the Wand, starting from the upper left letter and moving downward, one line per Name. Say, "In the Names and Letters of the Tablet of Union, I call forth the Powers of Spirit." Ring 2-1-2 with the Bell.

Intone the first Enochian call: "Ol sonf vorz jee, goho Yad Balt, lonsh kalz vonfo; Sobra zol ror ee ta naz-psad, grah ta mal-perj; dee-es holk kwah no-thoa zimz, od ko-ma ta nob-loh zeen; So-ba theel jeh-nomp perj aldee; Dee-es urbz o-bo-le jee re-sam; Kasarm o-ho-re-la taba Pire; Dee-es zon-renj kab erm yad-na. Pee-la far-zm znurza adna go-no Yad-peel, dee-es hom-to; So-ba eepam, loo eepa-mis; Dee-es lo-ho-lo vep zomd poamal, od bog-pa a-ee ta pee-ap pee-ah-mol od voh-an. Za-ka-re, ka, od zamran; o-do see-kle kwah; zorj, lap zirdo no-ko Mad, ho-ath Yai-da."

Raise the Wand on high and say, "Ye I evoke, oh Angels of the Celestial Spheres. Ye are the Guardi-ans of the Gates of the Universe and of this Magick Sphere. Be here present to shine your transcendent Light on this Cosmic Temple and all within. Achud Rash Achudotho Rash Yechudotho Temoratho Achud." Ring 3-1-3 with the Bell.

Go to the east and face south. Perform the Magick Circumambulation by giving the Sign of the Enterer and then walking around the Temple deosil three times, giving the Sign of the Enterer on passing the east each time. Imagine a current of white light passing through you each time this Sign is given. After three complete turns, return to the west side of the Altar in a deosil curve. A continuously flowing cylinder of subtle white force should have developed around the Temple.

Pronounce the Thelemic Declaration to dedicate every erg of magical energy generated in Temple to the Great Work of realizing the highest levels of consciousness in physical incarnation.

"Holy and Blessed art Thou, Oh Heru Ra Ha, Transcendent Glory that surpasses all things. May Your Infinite Love reach down to bless this temple, dedicated to Your service. Enlighten my mind and enliven my soul so that I may be better enabled to carry out Your Will, which is my Will, here on earth.

Thereby, let the Word of the New Law be pronounced once more so that the brilliant stellar consciousness may be further established in the soul of humanity.

Do what thou wilt shall be the whole of the law. I declare that the purposes and operations of this temple are dedicated to spreading the Law of Thelema throughout the world on all planes to further the evolution of life everywhere. Let this new Covenant, the Third Dispensation of humanity's transcendence, the fulfillment of all previous Laws, be realized in the Collective Consciousness for the healing of all races. Our individual Paths through infinite space are our personal Covenants with the Divine. So may we all come at length to full Self actualization. Love is the law, love under will."

Complete the opening by ringing a battery of 3-5-3 with the Bell, making eleven rings in total, and then make a statement of intent, declaring the purpose and intention of the rite, to initiate oneself into the office of Thelemic Adeptship.

First Point: The Quest of Truth

Take up the wand, raise it on high, and say, "Let the pentagram of Pure Will be forged by the powers of the elements. Let the spiral of power be built from the earth to the heavens with the calls of the mighty angels and by the Holy Name of Pure Magick." Replace the wand on the altar.

Go to the east and then walk deosil three quarters around the temple to the north. Take up the paten of salt, hold it before the Watchtower of Earth and intone the Enochian call for Earth. Feel all the powers of Earth charge the paten, making it a focus and emanater of that element. After finishing the call, say, "I have built the first rung of the spiral of power with the holy letter, He. I have gained the power of Will." Turn around, walk straight to the altar, and place the paten next to the pantacle. Feel the Earth powers charge the altar and the space above it. Walk deosil around the altar until reaching the west side, facing east.

Go to the east, take up the fan, and repeat the process done in the north but for Air. After finishing the Air call, say, "I have built the second rung of the spiral of power with the holy letter, Vav. I have gained the power of Knowledge." Turn around, walk straight to the altar, and place the charged fan next to the dagger. Repeat this process in the west for Water with "I have built the third rung of the spiral of power with the holy letter, He. I have gained the power of Silence." Then, in the south for

Fire, say, "I have built the fourth rung of the spiral of power with the holy letter Yod. I have gained the power of Courage."

Upon returning to the west side of the altar for the fourth time, take up the flask of oil and hold it before the Tablet of Union. Intone the second Enochian call of Spirit and feel all the powers of Spirit charge the oil, making it a focus and emanater of that element. After finishing the call, say, "I have built the fifth and final rung of the spiral of power with the holy letter, Shin. I have gained the power of Going. The earth and the heavens are united in the Grand Word of Integration." Slowly intone "Yeheshua" and replace the flask on the altar. Feel all the elemental forces on and around the altar focus on the flask so that this emblem of Spirit becomes a conduit through which all powers flow as one. Put on the Pentagram Lamen and say, "I declare the union of earth and heaven by the pentagram of integration in the Holy Name of Yod He Shin Vav He and by the powers of the Sphynx. My Will is pure." Take up the wand, raise it on high, and declare a general statement of your personal True Will. Replace the wand and ring five tones on the bell.

Raise your arms and hold out your hands. Feel yourself rising and say, "I have gathered the forces of my Will and of nature and fused them into infallible Gold. I have found the center of All, the center of the fourfold and threefold divisions of the elements. The world of the divided seven is spread out before my far wandering eye and I know myself to be utterly beyond it. Concern for the circumstances and appearances of the divided seven falls away as I exalt myself to the spotless realm of the integrated seven, the celestial world wherein the planets roam freely. The eternal nature of this astral is ever expanding, always unfolding new possibilities, transcendent far beyond the earth. 'I am uplifted in thine heart; and the kisses of the stars rain hard upon thy body.'"[4]

Perform the Greater Invoking Ritual of the Hexagram with Thelemic Keyword Analysis. Draw a hexagram appropriate to each planet indicated by the planetary tarot cards instead of at the four quarters of the magick temple. Start with Sol and then trace the heptagram in the order of the days of the week, ending with Saturn. Feel the infinite space of the cosmos woven around you by the planetary invocations. Return to the west side of the altar, facing east, for the final Thelemic Keyword Analysis.

"Behold! The worlds of the divided seven and the integrated seven are one. The Word of Creation is fulfilled. ABRAHADABRA!" Ring 3 – 5 – 3 with the bell.

Look down at the altar and then out to the far east. Say, "Here I stand in the midst of the stars and planets. The wondrous universe spreads out in all directions, eternal and continuous. Far off, I can see

---

[4] Liber Legis, chapter 2, verse 62

the earth, my old home. How small and insignificant it is, a frozen spark of the life power that is focused and emanated by all the stars in the cosmos. Yet, the tiny world of the divided seven is the place of my birth, the birthplace of humanity.

"I shall enter upon a quest for Truth to discover the ultimate nature, whose expressions are the blindness of earth and the vastness of infinite space. How can the undivided nature become divided? My only guides are my own True Will and the Law of Thelema, the most worthwhile ethic ever delivered to humanity. "Do what thou wilt shall be the whole of the law. Love is the law, love under will."[5]

Go straight to the south and take up the Staff. Return to the west side of altar and face east. Go to the east and face south. Hold the Staff in your right hand, out in front of you as if it shone with light. Hold the Pentagram Lamen in your left hand as it hangs around your neck. Circumambulate the magick temple once while saying the words of the quest, "Do what thou wilt shall be the whole of the law. I seek the Truth. Love is the law, love under will." over and over. Upon returning to the east, dip the Staff and continue for another turn around the temple while saying the words of the quest. Upon reaching the east a second time, face east, dip the Staff, let go of the Pentagram Lamen, and open the box containing Atu XIV. Take up the card with your left hand.

---

[5] Liber Legis, chapter 1, verses 40, 57

Gaze at the card and say, "I've finally discovered the Path of Truth. Unite all pairs of opposites to realize the one holistic principle which emanates each. The Naught emanates the Two. The Two mutually annihilate to return to The Naught. The cycle goes ever round and round but complexity builds with each turn. A universe is born."

Circumambulate the magick temple twice more as before, repeating the words of the quest while holding Atu XIV and the Staff. Upon returning to the east a second time, face east, dip the Staff, and open the box containing the Lamen of Luna.

Put it on and say, "The fabric of all matter and energy, all space and time, is woven of complexity. The web of life supports all minds and bodies. The whole of the universe is seen in everything, from the smallest to the greatest. My vision is made perfect."

Circumambulate the magick temple twice more as before, repeating the words of the quest while holding Atu XIV and the Staff. Upon returning to the east a second time, face east, dip the Staff, and open the box containing the Lamen of Sol.

Put it on and say, "I project my Pure Will through the universe and all becomes ordered at its touch. My rod is extended beyond the beyond. I shine with rays of my Light. My Word is made perfect."

Circumambulate the magick temple once more as before, repeating the words of the quest while holding Atu XIV and the Staff. Upon returning to the east, face east, dip the Staff, and open the box containing the Keystone of the Mysteries of Initiation. Place it in the far east, next to the Tablet of Union.

Return to west side of altar, face east, place Atu XIV on the east side of altar, and say, "The Quest for Truth is accomplished. The ultimate nature of all phases of manifestation is discovered. The life power, whose number and symbol is the holy letter He, weaves its web throughout all existence in spirals, one upon another. By the perfection of integration, by the perfection of vision, and by the perfection of the Word, the Totality is revealed. Celestial or terrestrial, coherent or transcendent, the Truth is that all that is, is consciousness. The created creates its own creator to bring itself into being. All that lives is a god in its own right. The supreme reality is the paradox of complexity. Deus est Cosmos est Homo." Slowly vibrate "ABRA-HADABRA."

"The cosmic and quantum Body of Light is complete."

Raise the Staff on high and solemnly say, "There are four gates to one palace; the floor of that palace is of silver and gold; lapis lazuli & jasper are there; and all rare scents; jasmine & rose, and the emblems of death. Let him enter in turn or at once the four gates; let him stand on the floor of the palace.[6]

"Ra-Hoor-Khuit hath taken his seat in the East at the Equinox of the Gods; Hoor in his secret name and splendour is the Lord initiating."[7]

---

[6] Liber Legis, chapter 1, verse 51
[7] Liber Legis, chapter 1, verse 49

Second Point: Crowning as Hierophant and Lord of the New Aeon

Remove all planetary, alchemical, and elemental emblems on the altar and around the temple except the oil, Holy Book, Lamp, bell, Keystone of the Mysteries, and the Tablet of Union. Change the altar cloth to white. Place a white and a red candle next to the book and oil, white candle to the north and red candle to the south. Place Atu XI, Lust, on west side of altar. Keep Atu XIV, Art, on the east side of altar. The Lamp in the east represents the station of Hoor Paar Kraat. Place the Staff in the southwest to represent the station of Ra Hoor Khuit. Place the Sword in northwest to represent the station of Heru Ra Ha. Place a chair in the east with an Egyptian style serpent crown and a red sash with Masonic badge on it, preferably with the Royal Arch design. Continue to wear the three lamens from the first point.

Stand at the west side of altar facing east, light the candles, and declare, "I, in my Body of Light, arise and enter into the realm of transcendent blue, the Stainless Abode beyond the celestial. I am Octinomos, the Eighth in the midst of the seven, the central principle of all mind and body, all being and becoming. The totality of presences is immediately about me as my heart sings of the fulfillment of Pure Will, the greatest of truths, 'There is no God but Man.'" Ring 3-2-3 on the bell.

"I am come to the Temple of the All wherein the Equinox of the Gods is taking place. I shall take my place as the new lord initiating."

Take up the Holy Book and read aloud *Liber Tzaddi*. Replace the Holy Book on the altar.

"I stand in the Hall of the Gods at the centermost altar. Before me is the station where the nascent god, Hoor Paar Kraat, abides in his egg of blue, perfectly protected, Hadit invested in a Khabs. To my right, behind me, is the station where Ra Hoor Khut, the hawk headed mystical lord of silence and strength, awaits his spell. To my left, behind me, is the station where Heru Ra Ha, the quintessence of all that is Horus, shines forth his fiery radiance to all the worlds. The great Gods of all creation are arrayed around the Hall to witness the advent of the New Aeon and the destruction of the old ways. Let the spell of Ra Hoor Khuit, the Crowned and Conquering Child, be raised."

Walk straight to the southwest, take up the Staff, and face east. March boldly to the eastern throne. Put on the sash with badge and the crown. Take on the godform of Ra Hoor Khuit. Sit on the throne, gaze out across the magick temple, and declare, "I have raised my spell. I have taken my seat."

Raise the Staff on high and declare, "I raise my double wand of power, the wand of the force of Coph Nia. The time of the twin warriors about the pillars of the world is at hand."

Hold out your left hand, palm open and facing up, and declare, "I have crushed an universe, leaving nothing."

Stand, raise the Staff and your open left hand on high, and declare, "The Word of Heru Ra Ha is complete. By the spell of my true Name, I raise the Word of the Mysteries of Initiation," Vibrate slowly, "A-BeRA-VAD-AB-RA."

Go to the west side of altar, facing east. Perform the Thelemic Keyword Analysis with great solemnity. Project Thelemic energy to all the worlds and spaces as Hierophant of the new aeon. Announce that a ray of your cosmic Light has returned to earth to take up the cause of Thelema according to your True Will.

Third Point: Reentry into the World as Ra Hoor Khuit

Restore all planetary, alchemical, and elemental temple appointments as in the opening. Leave the altar appointments of the Second Point on the altar. The new Hierophant remains dressed as in Second Point and sits on the eastern throne. Maintain the godform of Ra Hoor Khuit.

Reach out to the universe of space and time and declare, "I have come to take my office as Hierophant of the Aeon of Horus. Let all the worlds of consciousness harken to my Word."

Take the Holy Book from the altar and read chapter Three of *Liber Legis*. Replace the Holy Book on the altar.

"I declare that my True Will is done in this magick temple for the whole of the new universe. Let my Word be carried to its farthest reaches."

Go to west side of altar, face east, and ring 3-5-3 with the bell.

Closing:

Perform the banishing form of the Greater Ritual of the Hexagram as in the First Point. Then, perform the purification and consecration as in the opening. Close the Angelic Tablets as follows:

Go to the eastern tablet, Wand in hand, and say, "Let us banish the Powers of Air with the Great Eastern Quadrangle." Draw the banishing active spirit pentagram in black against a white background over the tablet, point to the center, and vibrate AHIH and EXARP. Draw the banishing Air pentagram in violet against a yellow background and vibrate IHVH. Draw the Kerubic sign of Aquarius with the Wand in violet within the Air pentagram and vibrate Raphael. Draw a golden cross over the Great Cross of the tablet from top to bottom and then left to right. Draw a widdershins golden circle around the cross. Point to the center and say, "In the names and letters of the Great Eastern Quadrangle, I banish the Powers of Air." Knock once with the Wand.

Repeat appropriate banishing formulas for the other tablets in the south, west, and north. Complete the circle and return to the west side of the Altar, facing east. Say, "Let us banish the Powers of Spirit with the Tablet of Union."

Draw the banishing passive and active spirit pentagrams over the Tablet of Union, using the colors and vibrating the Names as in the opening. Point to the center and say, "In the names and letters of the Tablet of Union, I banish the Powers of Spirit."

Perform the Magick Reverse Circumambulation by circling the Temple widdershins. Imagine a current of white light passing through you, counteracting the deosil current set up in the opening. After three complete turns, return to the west side of the Altar in a widdershins curve. The cylinder of subtle white force should be gone.

Raise the Wand on high and say, "I hereby give license to depart to any and all spirits that may have been attracted by this rite. Return unto your habitations and abodes, harming none on your way. Let there ever be peace between all of you and I and be ready to come again when called. For now, depart!" Knock forcefully with the wand on the altar.

Declare the Temple closed with a final statement of accomplishment and ring a battery of 3-5-3 with the Bell.

COMMENTARY TO THE THELEMIC ADEPT SELF INITIATION CEREMONY

This ceremony is intended as a recognition of years of magical work and spiritual transcendence. Anyone who performs it should have already achieved some level of consciousness of the states of mind and being described in the speeches herein. The goal of the operator is to create an elaborate context in which to understand the magical advances already made. The self made adept can then explore the new states of being implied by the magical journey undertaken in the ceremony. This commentary will clarify some of the more obscure details of the script.

The preparation and opening of the Thelemic Adept Self Initiation Ceremony is the same as that of the Enochian temple working specified in my previous book, *Enochian Initiation*, but with some additional symbols. The higher octave forms of the elemental weapons are used as well as the traditional implements to represent the mind and body of the macrocosmic Self, the Higher Self or Augoeides of Golden Dawn usage. The Staff, Chalice, Sword, and Lamp represent Fire, Water, Air, and Spirit, respectively. The altar as a whole is the higher octave symbol for Earth. These are the elements of the superconscious wholeness in which the adept lives and is aware. Realization of the macrocosmic

Higher Self is the classic prerequisite for initiation into the mysteries of adeptship and the celestial world of the higher magick.

Emblems of the three alchemical elements are placed in triangular formation around the temple for a more complete elemental presence in the magick to follow. This also overlays an implied triangle onto the cross of the classical elements, suggesting a threefold process to the fourfold universe. The triangle is often a stand in for the circle and so in this context, the element of time and cyclicity is added to the vastness of space and nature. Further, it is immediately evident that the cross and triangle have a common center on the altar, making this an eighth spiritual element for both elemental groups. The number eight plays another significant role in the temple setting of the second point, the Temple of the All beyond time and space. The reader may be reminded of the old Hermetic axiom, "As above, so below." The different planes of existence reflect each other, following certain sets of patterns which unfold in all settings and states of consciousness but in different ways.

Seven of the 22 tarot trumps, the major arcana cards, are placed around the temple at the points of an imaginary planetary heptagram. This is not to be confused with the Babalon form of the heptagram, which has a different significance than the planetary form. Each of the major arcana cards, the atus of Thoth, is attributed to one of the planets, elements, and signs of the zodiac, with two of them having two attributions. The seven trumps attributed to the seven classical planets are to be used in constructing this additional temple overlay to symbolize the vast, starry heavens in which the earth moves and has its being. Consult Aleister Crowley's, *Book of Thoth* for these Hermetic attributions and the shape of the planetary form of the heptagram.

Four boxes are placed in the east to hide the symbolic milestones of the Quest for Truth, which occurs in the first point. A golden pentagram lamen is placed on the altar to symbolize the psychic and spiritual wholeness that the adept achieves in preparation for this quest. The Holy Name of Pure Magick, the Grand Word of Integration, Yeheshua, also Yod He Shin Vav He, is also symbolized in graphic form. The opening can commence with these preparations.

The first point begins with a determination to purify the Will and build a spiral pathway from the earth to the heavens in order to achieve a transcendent state of magical being. Each element is visited in order from densest to lightest. The Enochian call for the Watchtower tablet is used to purify and perfect the element so that it can be incorporated into the spiral of power leading to the transcendent realm of the stars and planets. The corresponding letter of the Grand Word and the related Power of the Sphynx are announced to identify the magical integration of the psyche with climbing the ladder into the spotless realm of the astral plane. The pentagram of pure and perfect Will is completed as the adept is realized as a being of cosmic nature, at one with the stars and planets of eternal, infinite space.

The Supreme Invoking Ritual of the Hexagram is then performed to unite the planets with the configuration of the heptagram. The lines of the heptagram are traced as the adept moves from planetary tarot card to tarot card in the order of the days of the week. The macrocosmic Self is established and is united with the microcosm under the influence of the Word of Creation, ABRAHADABRA. The greater and lesser worlds complete each other in one grand reality, allowing the Pure Will to wield powerful creative magick.

A mystery is revealed at the climax of achieving perfection. The stark difference between the small, blind terrestrial world and the vast, free, starry cosmos of life, light, love, and liberty is observed in fullest detail. How could a creature born of the dark earth arise to the limitless abodes of the universe? How could the ubiquitous life power of all of space and time have created such a small, closed off world? The adept makes a decision to enter into a quest for truth to answer these questions, to discover the ultimate nature underlying the great and the small, the bright and the dark, to realize a yet higher attainment of perfection. This truth is well hidden in the totality of existence.

The adept's only guides through this mystery is her/his Pure Will and the Law of Thelema as stated in Aleister Crowley's *Liber Al vel Legis*. The Law of perfect freedom and autonomy has allowed the adept to discover her/his True Will and realize cosmic reality. The slave gods of the old aeon are overcome as the true nature from within all humanity becomes manifest among individuals. These personal and impersonal truths start the adept on the quest for even higher truth which will encompass all light and darkness.

The journey takes place by circumambulations around the temple, a symbolic wandering around the universe to look for the all encompassing truth of reality. A total of seven rounds are made to express the idea that the totality of the astral plane is searched. Gradually, the magical insignia of the adept are discovered, each with its own lesson about the truth and the corresponding perfection for having realized it. Eventually, the climax of the quest is reached with the discovery of the Keystone of the Mysteries, which declares the entire mystery and so accomplishes the quest. It is up to the adept to design and construct this ultimate expression of Truth according to the adept's total understanding of all things personal and impersonal, psychic and material. All subsequent magical effort should be guided by this cohesive comprehension, the cornerstone the adept's magical life.

In any case, this realization of totality should be consistent with the statements regarding the Thelemic ideals expressed in the final speech of the quest. The adept will have to make any necessary changes to these declarations if this is not the case.

Let the Thelemic magician use the supreme new aeon magical formula, ABRAHADABRA, to finalize the spell that confirms all mystical realization and initiatory growth. The Word of Creation is the Word of Initiation, the formula whereby the universe came into existence and the magician achieves transcendent states of being and becoming.

The supreme knowledge of all levels of creation brings the adept to a metalevel state, a consciousness beyond all matter, energy, space, and time, and yet encompassing them all. The cosmic Self and the subatomic, quantum Self become incorporated into one Body of Light capable of entering into any state at any scale of size as well as reaching beyond all the realms of unfoldment. This transcendent, transdimensional vehicle of most exalted consciousness perceives the call of the new aeon, the moment of its advent at the Equinox of the Gods according to *Liber Al vel Legis*. The ascension of Horus to the station of Hierophant in the Temple of the All is declared to prepare the adept for the next stage of this self initiation.

It is within this greater Body of Light that the adept arises and enters the Stainless Abode, the source state of all conditional existence. The spiral nature which constitutes the adept and all else in existence as one continuum of complex unfoldment is understood to be Octinomos, the eightfold principle whose pattern is echoed throughout the celestial and terrestrial worlds. It is the creative and enlightening principle that has always been conceived of as the solar-phallic power of the male horned god in his many manifestations. Aleister Crowley declared this to be the magick force in its pure form. The reading of *Liber Tzaddi* confirms the initiatory nature and purpose of the office to be filled. The adept can proceed to take her/his place as the Hierophant of the new aeon with this realization of purest, unconditioned Self, the power underlying all consciousness, life, and the material universe.

The advent of the Aeon of Horus, the Crowned and Conquering Child, takes place as Ra Hoor Khuit ascends the Hierophant's throne. The adept makes this step by uniting Ra Hoor Khut with Hoor Paar Kraat, the nascent god who is Hadit extended into a star. Chapter 2 of *Liber Legis*, the Hadit chapter, verse 49, states, "This is of the 4: there is a fifth who is invisible, & therein am I as a babe in an egg." The invisible fifth principle is the element of Spirit and Hoor Paar Kraat is figured as a babe in an egg of blue light. Also, chapter 2, verse 2, says, "I am not extended, and Khabs is the name of my House." Khabs is the ancient Egyptian word for star. Verse 8 says, "Who worshipped Heru-pa-kraath have worshipped me." Here is a direct statement of identity between Hadit and Hoor Paar Kraat. Uniting Ra Hoor Khut with this subtle principle adds the letter "i" to complete and raise the spell of Ra Hoor Khuit.

The adept, as the complete Horus, takes His station, puts on the serpent crown and sash of the Royal Arch mysteries of Freemasonry, and makes the appropriate declarations. The crown symbolizes the power and authority of Ra Hoor Khuit and the Royal Arch sash expresses that ultimate magick force of all truth which transforms a human being into a higher form of life.

The adept then raises the supreme and perfected Word of all creation, initiation, and magick. The H in ABRAHADABRA is advanced to the V, just as expressed by the Thelemic keyword, HERU. This mystery is given in *Liber Legis*, Chapter 2, verses 15 and 16. "For I am perfect, being Not; and my number is nine by the fools; but with the just I am eight, and one in eight: Which is vital, for I am none indeed. The Empress and the King are not of me; for there is a further secret. / I am The Empress & the Hierophant. Thus eleven, as my bride is eleven."

These obscure passages can be understood by the use of the keyscale numbers and Hebrew letter attributions of certain of the tarot trumps. Naught is identified with perfection in both chapters 1 and 2 of *Liber Legis* and Hadit declares himself to be perfect and nothingness. The tarot trump whose keyscale number is 0 is The Fool. Crowley identifies the symbol of the Fool with Harpocrates, that is, Hoor Paar Kraat, identified with Hadit as specified above. His number can be calculated to 9 as He – Daleth, H(a)D, 5 + 4. Note the absence of the Aleph, which the fools are unable to understand. These letters are identified in the old tarot decks with the trumps called, The Emperor or King and The Empress. Hadit states that these letters and concepts are not of him. His true name, understood by the just, the enlightened, is Vav – Aleph – Daleth, VAD. The related tarot trumps are The Hierophant, The Fool, and The Empress, and their keyscale numbers are 5, 0, and 3, which add up to 8. The numeric values of these letters are 6, 1, and 4, which add up to 11. Thus, Hadit's true name is 8 and 11 and, as The Fool, he is the Aleph in the midst, 1 and 0. He is the creative Octinomos and the unknowable cosmic nature at one with Nuit, infinite space and the infinite stars thereof. Together, they complete all of existence.

The first two syllables of the supreme and perfected Word are lengthened to three with an alternative breakdown of pronunciation. In Hebrew, the triliteral, BeRA, means creates or created. Also, AB means father and RA is the name of the Egyptian Sun God. The entire mystery word, A-BeRA-VAD-AB-RA, means Aleph creates VAD, root of the solar-phallus. The solar-phallus has been celebrated throughout human history in one form or another as the primary creator of all reality and life. Its significance in the human psyche has been described in detail by the psychologist, Carl Jung, and others of his school. This mystery word expresses the entire course of Hadit's realization from pure nothingness to the totality of existence. It is the core mystery of Freemasonry, Hermetic occultism, and all religion.

The advance from He to Vav is then formally ritualized by the performance of the Thelemic keyword analysis at the altar, the common center of all planes of existence, the backbone of reality. The adept will understand the elements of the HERU formula in the context of this ceremony from here on out. H will not only symbolize Nuit but the pentagram of integrated and pure Will whose touch brings order to chaos. E is Hadit as the serpentine Octinomos that creates and binds together all existence in one continuous order of being, the being of which the adept is an integral part and totality thereof. R is the adept's royal heritage, love, and power to work True Will on any plane soever, the crown of Ra Hoor Khuit. U is the adept's office as Hierophant of the new aeon, dispenser of Thelema in a new reality of perfect freedom.

The worlds of unfoldment share in this perfection as the new Hierophant projects a ray of her/his cosmic Light back to the tiny earth of human origin to further the establishment of Thelema on all planes. The extremes of reality have met. The newly realized and perfected adept takes up the Hierophant's throne and office in the world of the elements and declares the word of Ra Hoor Khuit. The whole ceremony is sealed with the eleven fold Thelemic ring of the bell. True Will has been accomplished in the magick temple. The adept may perform magick on all the planes of existence adventured in this ceremony.

SUGGESTED READING LIST

(* means important to the magician)

MAGICK

ALCHEMY AND HERMETIC MAGICK
Alchemy by Titus Burckhardt
The Hermetic Tradition by Julius Evola
The Alchemical Mandala by Adam McLean
The Kybalion by Three Initiates

Ceremonial Magick
The Candle of Vision by A. E.
Three Books of Occult Philosophy by Henry Cornelius Agrippa
The Magus by Francis Barrett

Crowley, Aleister
> *Book 4*, Parts 1 through 4, also *Book 4, Magick In Theory and Practice*, and *Equinox of the Gods*
> *Eight Lectures on Yoga*

The Magick of Thelema by Lon DuQuette
Introduction to Magic by Julius Evola

Eliphas Levi
The Magical Ritual of the Sactum Regnum
Transcendental Magic

Mathers, S.L.
Astral Projection, Ritual Magic, and Alchemy
The Book of the Sacred Magic of Abramelin the Mage

Regardie, Israel
Gems From the Equinox
The Golden Dawn
The Secret Inner Order Rituals of the Golden Dawn
The Tree of Life

Enochian Magick
The Vision and the Voice by Aleister Crowley
Enochian Vision Magick by Lon DuQuette
Enochian Initiation by Frater W.I.T.
The Enochian Magic of Dr. John Dee by Geoffrey James
The Complete Enochian Dictionary by Donald Laycock
Golden Dawn Enochian Magic by Pat Zalewski

GOETIC AND GRIMOIRE MAGICK
DuQuette, Lon
> *Aleister Crowley's Illustrated Goetia Angels, Demons, and Gods of the New Millennium*
> *The Key to Solomon's Key*
> My Life With the Spirits

Mathers, S.L.
> The Grimoire of Armadel
> The Key of Solomon the King

QABALAH
Crowley, Aleister
> *777 and Other Qabalistic Writings*
> The Book of Lies

> *The Chicken Qabalah of Rabbi Lamed Ben Clifford* by Lon DuQuette
> *The Mystical Qabalah* by Dion Fortune
> *The Sefer Yetzirah In Theory and Practice* by Rabbi Aryeh Kaplan
> The Kabbalah Unveiled by S.L. Mathers
> *The Qabalah* by Papus
> The Holy Kabbalah by A. E. Waite
> *Kaballah of the Golden Dawn* by Pat Zalewski

ROSICRUCIANISM AND FREEMASONRY
> *The True and Invisible Rosicrucian Order* by Paul Foster Case
> Duncan's Ritual of Freemasonry by Malcolm C. Duncan

A Rosicrucian Notebook by Willy Schrodter
Scottish Rite Illustrated by A Sovereign Grand Commander

TAROT

The Book of Tokens by Paul Foster Case
The Book of Thoth by Aleister Crowley, The Master Therion
Understanding Aleister Crowley's Thoth Tarot by Lon DuQuette
Mystical Origins of the Tarot by Paul Huson
The Tarot of the Bohemians by Papus

THELEMA

Crowley, Aleister
> *The Book of the Law*
> *The Book of Wisdom or Folly*
> *The Collected Works of Aleister Crowley*
> *The Heart of the Master*
> *The Holy Books of Thelema*
> *Konx om Pax*
> *Little Essays Toward Truth*
> *Magick Without Tears*

> *The Law is For All* by Israel Regardie and Aleister Crowley

MATHEMATICS

Fractals: The Patterns of Chaos by John Briggs
The Golden Ratio by Mario Livio
The Beauty of Fractals by H. O. Peitgen and P. H. Richter

The Mathematical Tourist by Ivars Peterson

PHILOSOPHY

Flatland by Edwin Abbott
The Doors of Perception/Heaven and Hell by Aldous Huxley

PSYCHOLOGY

Hillman, James
   A Blue Fire
   The Soul's Code

Varieties of Religious Experience by William James

Jung, Carl
   Man and His Symbols
   The Psychology of the Transference

Leary, Timothy
   The Game of Life
   The Psychedelic Experience

Lilly, John
   The Center of the Cyclone
   Programming and Metaprogramming In the Human Biocomputer

The User Illusion by Tor Norretranders

Reich, Wilhelm
  The Cancer Biopathy
  *The Function of the Orgasm

PHYSICS

CHAOS THEORY
  *The Quark and the Jaguar by Murray Gell-Mann
  *Choas by James Gleick
  A Different Universe by Robert Laughlin

Peat, F. David
  *Synchronicity: The Bridge Between Matter and Mind
  *Turbulent Mirror with John Briggs

Prigogine, Ilya
  The End of Certainty
  *Exploring Complexity with Gregoire Nicolis
  Order Out of Chaos with Isabelle Stengers

Cosmology
  Relativity by Albert Einstein
  A Brief History of Time by Stephen Hawking
  A World Without Time by Palle Yourgrau

THE HOLOGRAPHIC MODEL OF REALITY
  *Wholeness and the Implicate Order by David Bohm
  The Holographic Universe by Michael Talbot

THE PHYSICS OF CONSCIOUSNESS
Penrose, Roger
>   *The Large, the Small and the Human Mind*
>   **Shadows of the Mind*
>
>   *The Physics of Consciousness* by Evan Harris Walker

QUANTUM PHYSICS
> **Entanglement* by Amir Aczel
> *The Tao of Physics* by Fritjof Capra
> *The Elegant Universe* by Brian Greene
> **Quantum Reality* by Nick Herbert
> *Tapping the Zero-Point Energy* by Moray B. King
> **The Non-Local Universe* by Robert Nadeau and Menas Kafatos
> *Superstrings and the Search For the Theory of Everything* by F. David Peat
> *The Dancing Wu Li Masters* by Gary Zukov

FIRST FIVE RECOMMENDED BOOKS TO READ
> *The Mystical Qabalah* by Dion Fortune
> *The Golden Dawn* by Israel Regardie
> *Gems From the Equinox* by Israel Regardie
> *Enochian Vision Magick* by Lon DuQuette
> *Understanding Aleister Crowley's Thoth Tarot* by Lon DuQuette

Breinigsville, PA USA
04 March 2011
256985BV00001B/7/P